Did you know that . . .

- The way your handwriting slants reveals your ability to express emotion?

- Upper and lower loops give insight into imagination?

- Blacking out certain letters may indicate a problem with food or alcohol?

- The way you write your *m*'s and *n*'s can reveal whether you are an analytical, methodical, or intuitive thinker?

- The way you cross your *t*'s indicates your level of enthusiasm?

START CHANGING YOUR LIFE TODAY—
LEARN THE AMAZING SECRETS OF
GRAPHOTHERAPY!

REWRITE YOUR LIFE

D1603161

Rewrite
Your Life

SHEILA KURTZ, M.G.A.,

with Marilyn Lester

St. Martin's Paperbacks

REWRITE YOUR LIFE

ISBN: 0-312-95947-8

Printed in the United States of America

St. Martin's Paperbacks edition / August 1998

10 9 8 7 6 5 4 3 2 1

CONTENTS

ACKNOWLEDGMENTS

Rewrite Your Life is a special book for me because it allows me to put into writing the graphotherapeutic material that I have passed on to others. I'd like to thank, therefore, all of the graphotherapy clients who have crossed my threshold over the years. Their experiences have helped us both grow.

I would like especially to thank Terry Jackson. The wonderful results of our work together over the years particularly encouraged me to write this book. To Harvey Klinger and his thoughtful help and sense of humor; and to Heather Jackson, for seeing this project through. My thanks also to Barney Collier, a special friend who helped give form to this book. To Jean Creighton, a supportive neighbor and friend. To Eve, thanks for being my mother; and Amanda, Jared, and Daisy, and the rest of my family and friends who have never failed to give me support.

1
WHAT *REWRITE YOUR LIFE* CAN DO FOR YOU

CHANGE YOUR HANDWRITING, CHANGE YOUR LIFE. THAT IS A very powerful concept, and it happens to be absolutely correct. You can use your own handwriting to alter your behavior. The method is called graphotherapy, and I've been using it for years to help clients better their lives and achieve their goals. Using my graphotherapy method, you can actually see the changes in your handwriting and feel the effects in your life.

As a certified handwriting analyst and graphotherapist, I've helped people make important discoveries about themselves. What they had in common was a desire to improve the quality of their lives and a resolve to do it on their own. I wrote this book because of these successes. Many of my graphotherapy clients have gotten satisfying results from my method—and many had previously spent a lot of money on more traditional therapies without much benefit.

I wrote *Rewrite Your Life* so that you can pursue your quest for personal change with me as guide, mentor, and partner. I've included the most relevant information for your needs. When you follow the steps, spending just fifteen minutes a day on the exercises, you will begin to feel the differ-

ence in yourself in as little as a month. You can achieve
swift, specific personality changes, such as:

- raising self-esteem
- increasing concentration
- overcoming self-consciousness
- developing confidence
- sharpening success skills
- improving mental clarity
- beginning to eliminate fears

This book shows you how to achieve all this, and more.
By the time you finish *Rewrite Your Life*, you'll have formed
new behavior patterns through handwriting changes, creating a new knowledge base and awareness of your abilities
and capabilities. Best of all, you'll have formed strong internal beliefs about your self-worth.

WHAT'S IN A NAME

Graphotherapy is an outgrowth of graphology, also
known as handwriting analysis. Many practitioners prefer
the term *graphology* to *handwriting analysis* because it
sounds more scientific.

In the modern era, the methods of handwriting analysis
have been constantly researched, refined, and updated, but
in the last two decades, computers have enabled a more scientific method of analysis to be developed based on
advanced statistical methods. Because of this advancement,
many computer-literate practitioners use a new term,
graphonomy, which describes graphology augmented by or
studied through computer analysis, referring to themselves
as graphonomists.

WHAT GRAPHOTHERAPY IS ABOUT

Before there was Freud, before there was Jung, and before there was any kind of formalized psychotherapy, there was handwriting analysis—probably the oldest means on record (going as far back as the ancient Greeks) for studying human personality and behavior. The reason for this is simple and logical: Written words are the symbols by which we communicate.

Handwriting as a means of recording words has its own vocabulary in form and movement. In other words, writing strokes are forms in action. These strokes are what graphologists analyze to construct a picture of personality.

To understand this concept, and set the stage for graphotherapy, let's take a brief, very basic look at what graphology is and isn't.

When we learned to write in school, we were also learning to conform to a universal pattern of communication that becomes imprinted in the subconscious mind. Yet your handwriting is as unique as you are. Just as there are no two snowflakes alike, there are no two handwritings alike, although some may seem very similar. The uniqueness of your handwriting stems from the fact that when you write, your brain selects those parts of the overall pattern that reflect your personality, omitting the parts representing traits you don't have.

With maturity and life change, handwriting also changes to include different or unused parts of the unconscious pattern.

HANDWRITING IS REALLY BRAINWRITING

You see handwriting as language, a collection of words, composed of the letters of the alphabet, that communicates meaning. However, your brain perceives handwriting not only as language, which can be written or spoken, but also as a collection of symbols, which can be apprehended only through the physical action of writing.

Just as there are exercises for the body, graphotherapy provides exercises for the mind. There is a definite, brain–hand connection, and from a purely physiological perspective, graphotherapy can not only be explained but also shown to be highly effective.

The classic model of the brain likens it to a computer, with its predetermined, fixed circuitry. In this model, a baby is born with the brain fully defined in accordance with a master "brain blueprint" for all individuals. However, a new brain theory, advanced by Nobel laureate Dr. Gerald Edelman, speculates that the brain is actually an ecosystem that organizes itself before birth: The nerves, driven by a specific genetic imperative, arrange themselves, resulting in a *unique* brain circuitry that can never be predicted. After a baby is born, the brain continues to develop along the lines of its own evolutionary adaptation so that thought, memory, and consciousness develop to permit us to cope with the world.

What is the significance of this theory for graphotherapy? *It means that the brain is a work in progress, and the mind of every individual is unique. Therefore, every handwriting is correspondingly unique and individual.*

From a physiological point of view, the brain is part of the central nervous system. It's made up, in part, of about ten billion nerve cells, linked together and responsible for controlling all of our functioning. The billions of nerve cells receive and transmit information—electrical signals are sent from nerve cells to brain cells and to muscle cells (and vice versa), transmitted by chemicals manufactured in the brain. This two-way street makes graphotherapy possible. When you write, the signal is transmitted between your brain and your hand, through the brain stem, to the spinal column, along the nervous system, and to the muscle system, enabling you to pick up your pen and begin writing. Sending a different signal from the pen back to the brain with new instructions is graphotherapy.

THE SYMBOLS OF HANDWRITING

The individual strokes that make up letters are the symbols of handwriting.

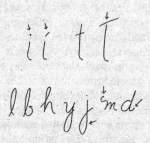

Some typical strokes are the *i* dot, the *t* bar, loops, hooks, and the individual components of the letters themselves.

While these strokes may look like handwriting to you, to a scientist or graphologist they are the means through which handwriting can be analyzed. Scientists have developed a standard recognition system with specific meaning assigned to each stroke.

The most popular recognition approach is called model-based stroke detection. In this approach, an analyst assumes that there is a set of uncorrupted strokes that are typical to a specific writer. Once an understanding of this writing is achieved, the model can be extended to generalized script writing. The usual method that identifies strokes is an energy-based line follower, meaning that an unbroken line segment is followed until it arrives at an ambiguous region (or junction). Energy minimization is applied to obtain the ideal traversal of the segment. The energy is calculated by considering a combination of factors that involve the image and model information. Matching of the traversed stroke with the model gives an estimate of the direction and results in a valid classification for unambiguous strokes, so that meaning can be ascribed to each one.

Yet handwriting strokes have no meaning in and of themselves; they function as the bridge between the conscious and unconscious minds and are the means by which graphologists interpret behavior. Your brain is the generator of writing; your hand is only following instructions. The result is that handwriting is a frozen moment—an act of will caught on paper—so each symbol/stroke can be interpreted by a graphologist in much the same way that a doctor reads and interprets an electrocardiogram. The strokes that symbolize personality, and that reflect our singular natures, are incorporated in the diverse and distinct ways people write. Handwriting mirrors personality and achievement traits. Graphologists can make evaluations about characteristics that may include a person's aptness for social adjustment, attitude toward material values, depth of intellect, range of emotions, and creative capacity. They would not make evaluations about gender, race, origin of birth, age, or right- or left-handedness because these elements are not personality traits and therefore cannot be reflected in handwriting.

GRAPHOLOGY IS A SCIENCE

Graphology is a science but not an *exact* science. It's actually a form of psychology, one that uses the evidence of handwriting to show human individuality.

It is the nature of handwriting that you can't fake it, you can't "pull a fast one." Because of the brain-hand connection, and because a person's true personality reveals itself in handwriting, graphology has long been used in police and detection work and in forensic science. Law enforcement officials and the courts have used the services of graphologists to solve crimes and provide evidence for trials—for example, a will that someone may suspect is a forgery, or an important signature that is in dispute. These graphologists are analyzing the handwriting not as a personality assessment but to ascertain, by examining the strokes, its authenticity. Graphologists also look at and assess ransom notes and other kinds of communications that might provide clues for solving a crime or mystery.

Not only can't you keep up phony handwriting for very long (try it!), but graphologists can clearly see signs that the handwriting has been disguised. How? There are stops and starts, dots and hesitations present in the writing. Under high-intensity magnification, the graphologist not only detects all this but also sees that the writing is actually drawn. In other words, the forger draws the personality traits (that are not his or her own) as opposed to creating them with the natural rhythm and flow of bona fide handwriting. The inability to fake handwriting is significant in this respect: whereas people can learn how to fudge certain psychological tests, such attempts are virtually impossible in handwriting analysis. Natural handwriting shows people as they really are. It's this feature of graphology that led to the development of graphotherapy, the psychotherapeutic branch of handwriting analysis.

DOODLING IS A FORM OF GRAPHOTHERAPY

To begin to understand graphotherapy, think of doodling. Doodling is partially a conscious act—the pen seems to take on a life of its own while the mind is concentrating on something else. People doodle in various situations, while on the telephone, during lectures, taking notes, or while compiling lists. Doodling is nothing more than an instinctual form of graphotherapy.

Doodles can be assessed by a graphologist in much the same way as handwriting samples and graphotherapy exercises, because doodles are comprised of strokes and are also symbols. For example, hearts may represent a romantic period, guns could indicate overt or repressed aggression, and vehicles might point to a need to get away. Geometrical shapes such as triangles, squares, and pattern formations often tell a lot about a person's thinking (organized, clear, efficient, purposeful). Repetitive shapes often indicate patience, perseverance, and a methodical, developed ability to concentrate. As you'll see, the key to the exercises is that they are made up, in part, of repetitive shapes and patterns, all designed to reinforce positive personality traits.

The science of studying doodles and other human graphic endeavors constitutes a new, burgeoning field of research called graphonomics, which is the convergence of computer science, behavioral science, cognitive science, neuroscience, education, and forensic science to provide insight into the analysis of the human graphic processes. Graphonomics permits researchers to implement and improve algorithms for script recognition and for diagnostic use in forensic, educational, and clinical settings. Advances in graphonomics will benefit professionals in the fields of computer science, pattern recognition, artificial intelligence, human-computer interaction, movement science, cognitive (neuro)science, experimental psychology, communication, education, neuropsychology, forensics, graphonomy and, of course, traditional graphology.

GRAPHOTHERAPY IS LIKE REVERSE PSYCHOLOGY

The point of graphotherapy is to use handwriting exercises specifically designed to maximize desirable personality traits—hence the change your writing, change your life concept. By doing the exercises you are retraining the patterns imprinted in your subconscious mind. On a physiological level, your thoughts and emotions emanate from your mind-brain. They are transmitted through the motor reflex muscles and emerge as strokes of handwriting, further defined by size, form, and pressure. You are, in other words, your own information superhighway, with the data capable of being transmitted from brain to hand and from hand to brain. Thus, graphotherapy uses a rational, thinking approach to change unproductive beliefs into productive ones. The handwriting exercises themselves serve as positive reinforcement during the process.

GRAPHOTHERAPY IS SIMILAR TO BIOFEEDBACK

Graphotherapy is also a form of biofeedback. Biofeedback is classically defined as any technique that allows you to monitor your own bodily functions in an attempt to alter those functions. In typical biofeedback training, electronic or mechanical instruments are attached to the body. They measure certain functions and through lights or beeps help the user control physiological processes that might bring on disorders such as stress, migraine headaches, tics, muscle tension, and so on.

Graphotherapy exercises help train you to control psychological factors that affect your behavior. There are no machines, lights, or beeps, but every time you do an exercise, your circuits are open, and the two-way brain-hand connection is delivering the information you need to make positive changes.

HOW GRAPHOTHERAPY CAN BE USEFUL TO YOU

Graphotherapy is a valid scientific tool that can comfortably change your life for the better, in a nonthreatening way. With graphotherapy, unlike many other self-help or therapeutic methods, you are in charge. You are in control of the process and able to turn your life around on your own terms. This is why you are your own best therapist. There's also no need to be anxious or alarmed. You can put yourself in your own hands with complete confidence that you're in command. Graphotherapy is entirely safe to do. You can't hurt yourself.

You should know you're not in for a bumpless ride. You do need determination and commitment (that's part of what we will be working on). You also have to take responsibility for yourself, with the realization that you may be the source of your own problems. That's okay. What we're going to do together is help you develop your strengths. When you strengthen your positive characteristics, you'll find there is

great joy in accomplishment and a sense of tremendous
pride in the work you've done. Ultimately, with consistency
and reinforcement, you'll develop your own personal tools
for success. It's my belief that all of us have it within ourselves to take command of our lives and to shape our own
destinies.

Those of you facing hurdles and obstacles, as well as
those of you who simply want generally to improve your-
selves, will learn that graphotherapy is a very effective
means for learning successful skills for living. Graphotherapy can help you find out:

- what motivates you
- your strengths
- your weaknesses
- what you can achieve

Graphotherapy has immediate practical benefits. You can
use it to:

- improve compatibility in your relationships
- reduce stress
- develop controls for addictive behaviors and bad
  habits
- switch careers successfully
- find satisfaction in the job or career you already
  have

Everyone has the need to find balance, and graphotherapy is the means to this end. All of us have the potential to
better ourselves and get more out of life.

WHY YOU *CAN* CHANGE YOUR BEHAVIOR

When I was studying graphology, my teacher and mentor
noticed that I, although a dedicated and good student, had a
problem keeping my focus. To help remedy this, I first had
to measure the slant in the writing with a plastic gauge to

determine the emotional structure of it. I measured one hundred upstrokes, which certainly was an exercise in diligence. A second approach to address this problem, to my surprise, was an assignment of handwriting exercises. This became my introduction to graphotherapy. After working the exercises for discipline and concentration, I found myself changing my study habits for the better. This improvement came about because I was able to feel the essence of the traits and take responsibility for my problem.

Right from the beginning, this self-therapy was such a logical experience that I knew I wanted to make graphotherapy the core of my professional life. And this I have done. I knew then as I know now that such a potent way to help yourself (and in such a relatively short time) should be made readily available. So as much as is appropriate, I encourage people to get off the psychiatrist's couch and take control of their own lives.

BELIEVE IN YOUR CAPACITY TO CHANGE

We all go through changes throughout life. Some changes are sociological rites of passage such as religious coming-of-age, adolescence, graduation, marriage, divorce, menopause, old age, and death. Other life changes are not so much prescribed but just seem to happen; they may appear to be simply consequences of living, or events that occur beyond our control. Still other changes are induced or consciously sought. Regardless of how or why change happens, the truth is that *change is a fact of life*.

Because change is inevitable, and many of us fight it, the next question to ask is: What are we afraid of? The answer usually is that we don't believe we have control over our responses. I believe we can control our responses to life in ways that will make us more successful. We've all been programmed to some extent by a variety of sources, including parents, schools, important authority figures, the System, and bitter or sweet experiences. What is unfortunate is that certain behavioral programs we are implanted with or are wed to are not productive for our particular personalities, and so they may cause incredible stress.

The aim of graphotherapy is to help you learn to recognize tendencies toward stress and strengthen positive behavioral traits. Since graphotherapy works with what's observable—your handwriting—the results are almost immediate. This is a therapy in which everything is "up front" and consequently can be short term. When you seriously undertake graphotherapy, your potential is quickly to do the work, learn the lessons, and move on.

REALIZE THAT YOU'VE ALREADY BEEN MAKING CHANGE HAPPEN

Your handwriting is an accurate reflection of your personality; it changes and undergoes transformations, just as you do. Such changes are clear evidence of what is happening to your psyche. They are a historic record. You can see this record for yourself by examining your own handwriting from years gone by. Get out some samples of your past handwriting. Look them over carefully and compare them to the way you write today.

Chances are you'll see differences in the way you used to write compared to the way you write now—and the older the samples, the greater the observable changes are likely to be. You'll also notice that many of the strokes in your handwriting have stayed the same because there haven't been changes in those traits.

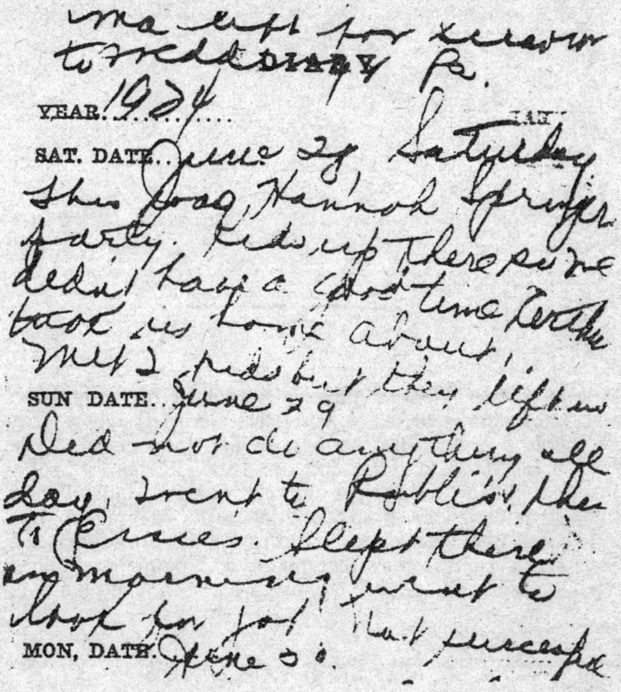

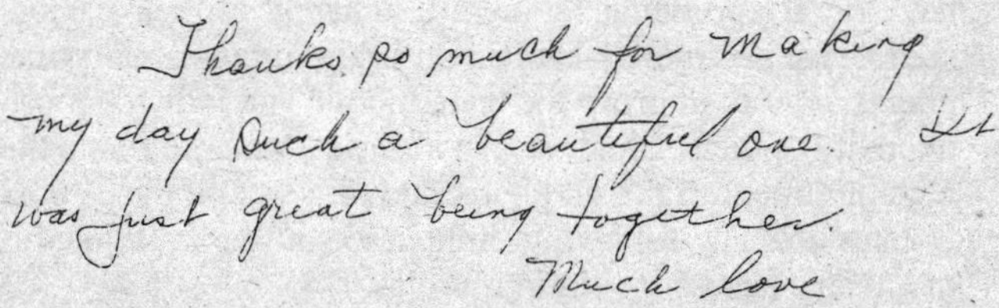

[Handwritten sample from 1924, partially legible:]

ma left for _____
to _____ Pa.
YEAR 1924
SAT. DATE June 28 Saturday
thus Joag, Hannah _____
_____ Kids up there so we
didn't have a good time _____
back as home about _____
_____ _____ but they left us
Did not do anything all
day, went to Publics, then
to Crises. slept there
my morning went to
look for jol. Not succeed
MON. DATE June 30.

[Handwritten sample from 1986:]

Thanks so much for making
my day such a beautiful one. It
was just great being together.
                    Much love

The handwriting on top is from 1924. The bottom sample is from the same individual writing in 1986. There are several differences, but the bottom one is more spacious and fluid, indicating a more "open" personality.

In 1969, Richard Nixon's signature (top) shows a strong sense of self in its relative clarity. The large capitals *R* and *N* also show a striving for recognition. In early 1974 (middle), just during the Watergate scandal, Nixon's signature has deteriorated, indicating a significant loss of self-confidence. By late 1974 (bottom), after he was forced to resign the presidency, the signature is barely recognizable; Nixon's confidence was so shattered that there was almost nothing left of it.

THEY DID IT—SO CAN YOU

Clients come to my office for different reasons. Some have family problems; some are unhappy in their careers; some have destructive habits they want to break. Corporate clients want to improve the team morale and individual productivity of their employees. In all cases, we have found that a commitment to the graphotherapy process produces positive results. The following three case studies are typical of the many success stories in my files.

Matthew Curtis*, trained as an electrical engineer, was being interviewed for a managerial position at a major electronics firm. While submitting his handwriting and being interviewed, Matt confided to me that it had always been his dream

*All names in *Rewrite Your Life* have been changed to protect privacy and client confidentiality.

to be a shoe designer. In looking at Matt's handwriting, I found that he indeed had the creativity and the potential to make his dream a reality. Among other positive traits, his handwriting was full of large lower loops, showing creativity and imagination; and breaks showing a wonderful intuitive sense:

I am trying to gather my resources together to explore some

The large lower loops in Matthew's y's and g's show creativity, while the breaks between the letters show intuition.

Encouraged, Matt began graphotherapy, primarily to get himself "unstuck." The creativity was already within him—he needed help with his goals and with his level of enthusiasm for pursuing his goals. I gave him several exercises to strengthen enthusiasm and goal setting (see pages 102 and 170), yet time was of the essence. Matt had just one month to decide whether he would accept his new position in the electronics firm, or "follow his dream."

Fortunately, the therapeutic results of graphotherapy, with its potential for immediate feedback, gave Matt the information he needed to make his decision. Matt opted for the shoe business, pursued his goal, and became a successful designer in the trade. In fact, he was so buoyed by the graphotherapeutic process that he placed his scripted signature on the sole of every boot and shoe that he designed—that was his trademark.

Sam Couf was one of my first graphotherapy clients. In fact, it was his success that encouraged me to pursue graphotherapy as the core of my career. Sam was interviewing for an important sales position and showed evidence of highly effective sales and communications skills. The problem was that he was cut from the final list of applicants, even though I could see he was the most suitable person for the job.

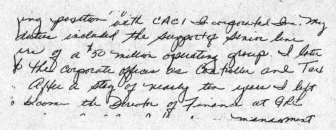

Sam's writing is full of confusion, seen in the way the words overlap and run into each other. This sample reflected his temporary emotional crisis and lack of focus.

What, then, was impeding him? Sam confided that he was in the midst of a complicated divorce, which was causing him tremendous stress and loss of focus. As a result of this life situation, Sam wasn't able to allow his natural strengths and talents to come across. Sam's problems didn't require long-term counseling, and in graphotherapy we were able to work effectively with a few basic exercises for relaxation (see page 74) and concentration (see page 85). As he mastered these, he learned to control his reactions to stress and regain his focus. I also encouraged him to resurrect his sense of humor. Sam did not get the job that initially brought him to me, but he was soon able to find a position that allowed him to use his skills and achieve success.

Celia Joff was a young woman with problems that had been building over the years. She had been in traditional therapy on and off with little result, and was eager to undertake graphotherapy. Basically, Celia didn't have the skills required to make traditional therapies a success. Although quite intelligent, she had a problem processing information, and lacked the mechanism to absorb and interpret data quickly. Graphotherapy is, however, a process that is tailored to individual needs. My program allowed her to work at her own pace, permitting her to absorb the information slowly, in a nonthreatening setting.

· I mentioned the possibility
of my mother coming to visit

If at first you don't succeed,
try, try again.

Here is the handwriting sample
you asked me to send you. I hope
it's what you want.

I can't thank you enough for being
helping me as you have. It has
good journey if a long and inten

The top sample is Celia's handwriting as I first analyzed it. The second sample belongs to her mother, and the third one below that is from her brother. Notice how the three samples lean to the left, indicating difficulty in dealing with emotions. All three also show repression in the way the n's and m's are written. The bottom handwriting sample is Celia's today. Notice how the slant is to the right, reflecting the tremendous emotional release she experienced as a result of her therapy. Celia's m's and n's also are freer and no longer indicate repression.

Since Celia lived in the Midwest, two thousand miles from my office in New York City, our first meeting was on the phone, but Celia soon decided to come to New York once a month for a one-on-one session. In between this counseling, I gave her exercises and "homework" to do. At first Celia was able to handle only fifteen minutes of personal consultation. Eventually, as she began to open up with less fear, her sessions lengthened, sometimes lasting for ten hours at a time. I included her in many of my business and personal situations that arose each time she visited. This allowed her to watch me handle some tough situations, and the outcomes and results of some of them truly amazed her.

We began with Celia's strong traits first, strengthening and reinforcing them so that they would become even stronger, helping her cope with the tougher work ahead. Our sessions were taped, and on that tape I included exercises for her to do in between our meetings (which we'd review in the next session before starting any new work). Celia's therapy was unusually long-term, lasting several years, but her problems were complex, stemming from childhood. In fact, part of the therapy included examining the handwriting of other members of her family. These illustrated clearly the patterns and behaviors that she was dealing with, which had been passed on within the family and from which she wanted to break.

This phase of the graphotherapy was a great help, because it showed Celia visually that she was part of an ongoing dysfunction, and that she wasn't imagining her problems or blowing them out of proportion. For example, women in her family were encouraged not to strive and to expect little return from life. As a result, Celia, like most women in her family, had low self-esteem and poor motivation for betterment.

Yet Celia had personality traits that allowed her to break the chain. Strengthening these traits posed no problem. It was later in therapy that she began to confront the problematic parts of herself. In performing the exercises during this phase of the work, she frequently felt conflict, doubt, depression, and anger. But the strong elements of her personality allowed her to press on and improve. Success built on success, giving Celia increased enthusiasm and commitment to the process. At one point, on a trip to southern California, Celia found herself experiencing an earthquake. She was very frightened, as she couldn't leave the building, and knew how important it was for her to relax and get through this scary turbulence. She remembered her graphotherapy exercises specifically for relaxation purposes. Celia worked constructively with an uncontrollable situation, keeping her mind focused and her stress minimized, activities that would have been closed to her prior to graphotherapy.

Eventually Celia felt strong enough to end our sessions together, which we did on a beautiful mountain in Arizona. This was a special journey for Celia, and I was there to share it with her. She not only had traveled a long distance to wholeness but also took with her the tools to keep working toward growth and success on her own.

Today Celia has her dream job of working as a fashion editor. This was one of her fantasies and eventually appeared as a visualization that she ultimately made happen. When she began her graphotherapy she was so stuck in her problems and had so little confidence that she was barely able to keep any job. People who knew her then would never have believed that she would emerge as a very successful, self-assured woman in a rewarding career and truly happy for probably the first time in her life.

CREATE YOUR OWN NEW REALITY

Cognition can be defined as awareness through thought, belief, or perception. In terms of personality, cognition deals with self-perception and personal beliefs. In graphotherapy, our aim is to eliminate those personal beliefs, statements, and programs that are limiting. We do this by creating a new set of realities about yourself. You have the ability through the power of your own thinking, intellect, creativity, and will to build and fashion your own life. Celia Joff's story is living proof of this.

We make life choices that fit our self-beliefs, and we all have limiting beliefs about ourselves, some of them so deeply rooted as to be subconscious or unconscious—that is, second nature. This is why we must eliminate or change the statements we make about ourselves that don't advance us. Here is a small sample of the many kinds of limiting beliefs and statements we might impose on ourselves. How many do you identify with?

- I'm not good enough.
- "They" are better than I am.
- "They" know more than I do.
- That's just the way life is.
- No one really understands me.
- I'm too (fill in the blank: sensitive, overweight, tired, old, young, etc.) to be effective.
- I was never given love.
- I can't.
- No one told me how.

Obviously, you can see that all of these statements block a person's effectiveness and capacity to achieve.

GRAPHOTHERAPY AND COGNITION GO HAND IN HAND

Graphotherapy, while using handwriting as a means of helping you make positive changes, encompasses cognitive processes as well. Cognition is the process by which we can know; it includes memory, perception, attention, reasoning, imagining, thinking, judgment, and speech. No one can really explain exactly how cognition works (although there are many theories on the subject), but we use it in graphotherapy to replace unproductive behaviors with productive ones. In other words, the exercises work cognitively to help you:

- determine your own life
- shape your behavior
- attack problems on a conscious level

THE POWER OF BELIEF

A study conducted by Jana Mossey and Evelyn Shapiro at the University of Manitoba, Canada, in the 1980s shows how beliefs affect our lives. Three thousand people age sixty-five or over were asked to rate their health on a scale ranging from poor to excellent. Simultaneously, each person was rated objectively by the experimenters based on medical records. The study found that those in objectively poor health who rated their own health as good had a higher chance of survival than those people in objectively good health who rated their own health as poor. The conclusion of the study was that what we believe about ourselves matters—so much that it literally affects living or dying. *Graphotherapy works with what you believe about yourself, which is why it has the potential to help you effectively take control of your life.*

It's not important to know how we got our limiting beliefs, or even why we cling to them. What is important is what we do about them, for they keep us from achieving success. Always remember that movement toward growth and fulfillment is primary in human beings. You can create a terrific new reality for yourself—and you deserve to do it.

2
WHAT GRAPHOTHERAPY FEELS LIKE

BEFORE I TELL YOU ANYTHING MORE ABOUT GRAPHOTHERAPY, I want you to experience it right away and feel the power of it. After you've done these preliminary exercises, you'll not only know intellectually what I'm sharing with you, but you'll also know it on an experiential, feeling level. Here is your first exercise.

EXERCISE 1

Get a paragraph of a friend or associate's handwriting. Copy it as exactly and precisely as possible (don't trace!), stroke for stroke, preferably using that person's pen. After completing the paragraph, copy the samples on the right. Mark off the ones that feel the most comfortable. Would you like any of these people to be your friend or business partner? Why?

Best Wishes

Greetings.
I'd. be much obliged
if you could mathe

surprise and gift it was, when Peter Beard first
s of Isak Dinesen's beloved Kamante. I had not
his drawings was like touching a talisman that

Before you
Judge Me, Try

You have a fine
and of my know you

Copy each of these handwriting samples as closely as
possible. How did it feel to do this exercise?

As you're writing, pay close attention to what you are doing and what you are feeling. When you've finished:

- Ask yourself how you felt when you were trying to write like someone else. Did you feel tense or tight? Free or loose?
- Write down exactly how you felt.

Important Instruction: Get a notebook and dedicate it to your work with this book. Your notebook will be the place you write down your feelings, thoughts, and the events of the day. Your notebook will be your diary and an important ally in the graphotherapy process. It will also be a road map that will show you how far you've come from your starting point.

Back to the samples you just copied. Don't be surprised if you felt quite different in some way, even disoriented or disconnected. I've conducted this experiment hundreds of times in my classes, at my seminars, and in my private counseling sessions, and each time the result was the same: Participants have intense feelings about the exercise, at times feeling at odds with it and at other times feeling great. The reason is simple: When you copy someone else's handwriting you're actually putting on someone else's personality. In your writing about the exercise, you'll see that in reality what you have done is to describe someone else's personality traits.

The personality that isn't yours sometimes may be, but frequently isn't, a comfortable fit. After all, it's not you, but it does give you a feeling about the other person—his or her stress level, humor, thinking. *The lesson of this exercise is: You are what you write.*

FYI: The handwriting samples provided on page 23 are from Donald Trump, John Kennedy, Jr., Jacqueline Kennedy Onassis, Michael Jackson, and Dan Quayle.

EXERCISE 2

This exercise is a taste of the exercise program you'll begin very soon. Begin by sitting comfortably at a desk or table and using a pen you especially like. Now, on a sheet of unlined paper, copy this illustration. Fill up at least a page, writing a line at a time, without lifting your pen from the page. Let your hand move across the page in an easy, fluid motion, making sure that even when you break to start a new line you still maintain the rhythm and flow.

Pay close attention to how you feel as you write. Get into yourself. Make yourself part of the experience. Open up your senses and be aware. In your notebook, answer these questions:

- How do you feel now?
- Did you notice a change?
- What kind of change?
- Did you feel more relaxed at the end of the exercise than at the beginning?

This is a graphotherapy relaxation exercise. If you are open, you may feel this exercise on a deep level, for it's also able to trigger feelings of expansion that ultimately allow you to broaden your horizons. Depending on your level of self-awareness, receptivity, and openness, you may feel the effects of the exercises immediately. Or you may need several sessions to realize the effect the exercise is having on you.

If you didn't feel a difference doing the exercise, try it again, this time allowing yourself to be more conscious of the process. This is a very powerful exercise. Whether you are aware of it or not, results are taking place.

EXERCISE 3

Graphotherapy relaxation exercises can help you keep stress levels low. They also help you prime your mind and make it more receptive to the exercises that are specifically designed to open up your mind. Now that you've practiced, do this exercise with an even greater intent to become part of it and feel the effect it is having on you. Fill up a sheet of unlined paper with this illustration. As you draw the waves, maintain the rhythm and flow. Think about musicality and dance. When you are finished, write down how you felt while doing the exercise.

If you didn't feel a difference, try it again. This time focus your attention on how your hand moves, how hard your fingers are gripping the pen, and the oceanic rhythm of the waves. Be aware of yourself as you think and move your hand across the page. Repeat this exercise often for best results.

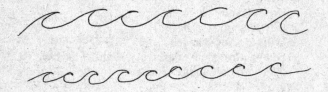

3
PRELIMINARY EXERCISES:
GETTING TO KNOW YOURSELF

THIS CHAPTER IS ABOUT GETTING TO KNOW WHO YOU ARE. THESE exercises comprise a tour of *you* through a guided graphology evaluation and assessment. We begin with you from your own "I" point of view.

If you recorded your conversations over a twenty-four-hour period and then listened to the playback of the tape, how many times would you hear yourself say the word *I*? And for that matter, have you ever heard anyone refer to himself or herself in any way other than *I*? What would you think of someone who referred to himself or herself in the third person? You'd undoubtedly think that person odd. The fact is, the only acceptable way to give reference to yourself in our culture is in the personal pronoun *I*.

This personal pronoun symbolizes the self and, in handwriting analysis, one's self-concept. It helps you answer the question, "Who am I?" It is the gauge of where you stand in time, an indicator of your personal worldview, and a reflection of the uniqueness of self. Often, it doesn't even match the rest of a person's handwriting, as this sample shows.

I wish that it was summer so that

Notice how the slant of the *I* is very different from the slant of the rest of the letters.

The slant of the *I* is symbolic of the way you present yourself to the world—the outgoing you. In this context, we can see in what time frame the self lives:

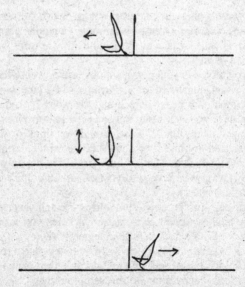

The vertical line represents the present. Thus, the area left of the vertical line represents the past, while the area to the right of it is the future.

The *I* slant represents your emotional attitude toward your social environment as follows:

- left *I* slant = a repression of forward movement, resistance to put self out, and a tendency to hang back and size up situations while still living in the past
- vertical *I* slant = controlled reactions
- right *I* slant = feeling free to forge ahead; going out in the world easily

Because the personal pronoun *I* reflects your self-image, the way you write it frequently changes when self-image does, as this case study shows. Dana Howell was coping with a mother who acted out her many problems on her daughter. Dana's father, a support and ally, had died many years before, leaving Dana (an only child) to deal alone with her mother. The mother was negative, criticized almost everything Dana did, and generally exerted such influence on her that Dana was psychically held back from reaching her full potential. I worked with Dana on this issue, using a variety of graphotherapy exercises, and we made great strides. Yet when our sessions together ended, despite the progress, her *I* still reflected the fragmentation she felt toward her mother. Her *I* still leaned way to the left, toward the past and in the region of unresolved emotional response in regard to her self.

Some years later, I became reacquainted with Dana. To my delight, she was now writing her *I*'s with a slight slant over to the right, so I knew that she finally had resolved her problems about her mother. Her mother had passed away several years before. Dana had continued to work on self-understanding and kept her graphotherapy exercises as an important part of her quest.

In conversation, Dana revealed that she hadn't noticed *when* her *I* changed. She told me she tried, as an experiment, to write her *I* the old way and became physically nauseated! Dana was now in balance. There is much useful information to garner from the personal pronoun *I*. You are right in front of yourself every time you write an *I*.

The hotel was much better than I expected. I would recommend it to anyone, even you-know who! It was comfortable and the service was as you'd expect in such a place.

Sheila;

It was terrific to see you again! I'd love to meet you for lunch sometime soon. I'll give you a call soon and we can make a date.

All the best —

D—

Dana's *I* in the top sample shows unresolved feelings about her parents, in this case her mother. Notice how the *I* leans toward the left but the rest of the writing does not. In the sample on the bottom, the *I* shows that Dana has come to terms with this issue. The *I* has become a single, firm standing stroke that no longer leans to the left.

EXAMINE YOUR OWN *I*

The successful development of a confident self is proportionate to the extent to which you become conscious about yourself, choose a frame of mind, and act with purpose. Keeping this in mind, as well as the fact that there are many traits in graphology that reflect your entire personality, I want you to study the types of *I*'s shown in the *I* chart and compare them to the way you write your *I*.

I CHART

 This is the learned-in-school *I*. People who write this *I* tend to be conventional and traditional in mind and habit. They live their lives as they were taught early on to live them.

 A single, unadorned straight line, or a straight line enclosed with cross bars, heading off in any direction indicates people who are direct, dislike wasting time, and seek the shortest distance between two points. Such people like to streamline. When they are creative, they often get their dreams to come true.

 A disproportionately large *I* formation signals overcompensation for feelings of limited self-worth.

 A very small yet well-formed *I* indicates socially modest sorts who can understand the power of inhibition.

 I in the lowercase, when used as a personal pronoun, indicates inhibition carried to excess. Such writers may often feel "the lowest," and they allow other people to see them that way.

 A small, isolated, subjugated little *I* indicates a form of mental depression. This *I* can be expanded with understanding and time.

A circle around the *I* is a form of emotional safety bubble that protects the writer from the world. Like any bubble, it easily bursts, often leaving the writer unprepared for the harshness of realities.

A muddy, blobby, narrow *I* signifies inner tensions and anxieties that are seldom relieved by moments of comfort or tranquility. Fortunately, it is one of the "treatable" *I*'s.

A theatrical *I* is made by writers who enjoy showiness in life.

An *I* made with thin, thready lines signals an apparently rootless state. Such writers tend to be blown with the winds and pulled by the tides.

A shaky, corrugated *I* indicates a physical or neurological malfunction that ought to be looked into and corrected. If this form appears in your writing, a checkup visit to a medical physician is advised.

Now do the following:

- Pick out the *I* that most closely matches your own on the chart.
- Write down your thoughts and feelings about the way you write your *I*.

Next, answer these questions in your notebook:

- Are you surprised at the comparison?
- Do you agree with it? Why or why not?
- Would you rather have another I? Why?

Read over the thoughts you've written down. If you are dissatisfied with any of them, remember that this book is about changing dissatisfaction into self-acceptance. So, as your sense of self unfolds in a more significant manner, you'll become better able to express your true self and reach the goals you visualize.

UNDERSTAND *WHY* YOU FEEL

There is a close connection between what we tell ourselves, how we feel, and what we believe to be reality. Are your feelings consistent or dissonant with your beliefs and actions? You must examine this, which is why I encourage you, as you do the exercises, to pay attention to your feelings before, during, and after them. The following case study is an excellent example of how feelings, beliefs and actions can become dissonant.

Allen Edwards was a successful bond trader and multimillionaire who had every material comfort imaginable but whose personal life was in chaos. Allen was unskilled at forming and sustaining personal relationships. He'd had two marriages, and after each one ended he told himself the reason for the failure was that his business life had interfered. This was partly true, because Allen made it so. What was more to the point, however, was that Allen refused to acknowledge his inability emotionally to handle a relationship.

[handwritten text, a rendering of the closing of the Gettysburg Address]

for us, the living, rather to be dedicated here
to the unfinished work which they who fought
here have of thus far so nobly advanced. It
is rather for us to be here dedicated to the
great task remaining before us — that from these
honored dead we take increased devotion to
that cause for which they gave the last full
measure of devotion — that we here highly
resolve that these dead shall not have died
in vain — that this nation, under God, shall
have a new birth of freedom — and that
government of the people, by the people, for
the people shall not perish from the earth.

Allen's handwriting slants to the left, indicating that he has
difficulty communicating and expressing his emotions.

With a prospective third wife on the horizon, Allen decided
he needed help. I could see by the leftward slant of the handwriting that Allen's main problem was difficulty in constructively expressing and directing his emotions. He didn't know
how to communicate with women, and he didn't want confrontation. Over a six-month period, working mainly on these
issues, primarily by giving him exercises on opening up and
overcoming narrow-mindedness (see pages 96 and 148), Allen
began to make new statements about himself and his beliefs.

Allen's program was changing. He came to realize that his marriages hadn't failed because business got in the way, but because he himself got in the way. He was able to take responsibility for his actions, begin to communicate, and handle confrontation. After five years, with a revised set of beliefs and feelings, Allen is still married to his third wife, who, he feels confident, will be his last. With new insight and skills, Allen was able to reconcile his relationship with his eighty-one-year-old mother, with whom he had had no communication for more than thirty years.

UNDERSTAND YOUR EMOTIONAL SELF

A fundamental part of your personality is your style of emotional response, which is indicated by the slant of your handwriting. The slant represents a basic desire, or lack of desire, to share our thoughts and feelings. It is also a sign of action and reaction. The slant is often called the emotional quotient or the measure of expression. Individual expression begins at the extreme left tilt and arcs to the extreme right tilt. Slant defines your personality type (see the case study below).

Our emotional structure is the most significant part of who we are. How we respond emotionally in situations is very revealing. Are we impulsive, objective, emotionally withdrawn? By measuring the slant of the handwriting we can assess our own structure as well as that of those with whom we interact. This is useful when trying to determine compatibility in personal as well as business relationships.

When in the Course

The left slant tilts into the past—a powerful force. Emotions may be held at bay. Sometimes the individual is self-absorbed.

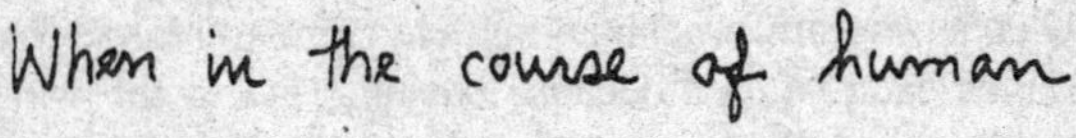

When in the course of human

The vertical slant indicates an objective mind, sometimes detached from the emotions.

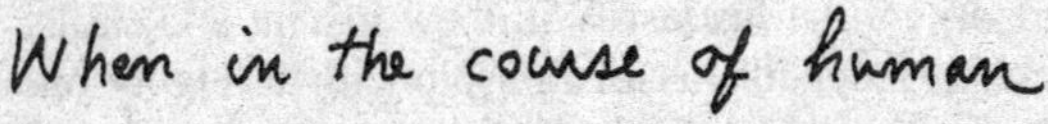

When in the course of human

The slant that is slightly to the right is a "feeling" slant; emotions are usually under control.

When in the course   *When en the course*

Multiple slants in the same handwriting, if moderate (left), � versatility. When extreme (right), there are heavy-duty mood swings.

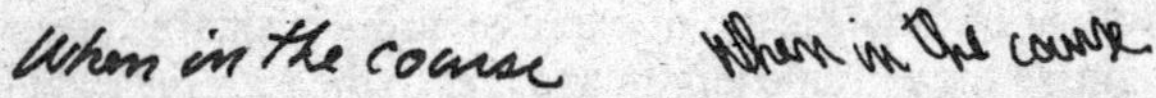

When in the course   *When in the course*

An extreme right slant (left) can indicate hysteria. An extreme left slant (right) indicates emotional withdrawal.

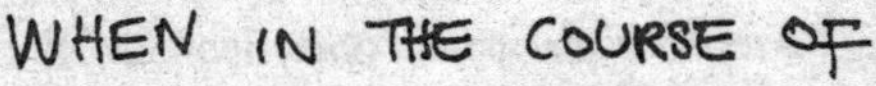

WHEN IN THE COURSE OF

Box printing reveals no emotional pattern. The writer is trying to hide something, usually something perceived as "terrible."

Amanda James came from a strict upbringing in which any expression of emotion, especially in public, was actively discouraged. Her parents weren't demonstrative, and rarely did she receive physical contact past her babyhood. To the outside world, Amanda appears to be cold and unconcerned. Yet her writing slants all the way to the right, indicating an intensely emotional person. The discrepancy stems from the fact that Amanda suppresses her emotions and has developed control mechanisms to do so. These controls show in the handwriting in tight, repressed *h*'s, *m*'s and *n*'s, and as very light pressure, indicating that Amanda chooses to operate on the surface. She has developed the ability to move from one situation to the next without dwelling on the emotional implications of any of them.

I am acquainted with Amanda only through her handwriting sample. Amanda did not choose to enter counseling, so I can only speculate on how graphology might help her reach her full potentials in life. For example, graphotherapy might help her:

- attain an understanding of her emotional structure and how she is covering it up
- provide balance to her emotional processing
- furnish opportunities to more consciously express her true self

Most of my friends from college have moved away from home and are scattered all over the country. There's not much time to be in touch with

Amanda's writing slants all the way to the right, indicating that she should be very emotional, but she doesn't appear to be. The reason is that Amanda has developed "controls" seen in the very light pressure of the writing and the tightly formed *n*'s, *m*'s, and *h*'s (repression).

KNOW YOUR PERSONALITY TYPE

There are five personality types, which I call graphotypes. They are the:

1. Introtype
2. Supratype
3. Supratype Plus
4. Extrotype
5. Varitype

An **introtype** has a leftward-leaning slant, which indicates some level of difficulty in expressing innermost feelings and emotions. Depending on the rest of the handwriting, an introtype could be someone who is perceived as cold and uncaring, or someone who simply doesn't easily communicate or express his or her feelings. Introtypes fear confrontation and open up at their choosing or only when forced to do so. It is difficult for them to feel trusting toward others and they are basically very private people. On the surface, introtypes may appear to be outgoing, but they are usually emotionally withdrawn.

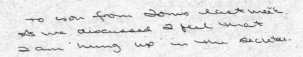

The introtype's handwriting slants to the left.

A **supratype**'s slant is straight up and down, which indicates that the emotions are under control. A supratype is likely to remain calm in an emergency, and seems to be able to handle emotional situations with practicality.

When the handwriting slants slightly to the right, the personality type is **supratype plus**. These individuals are considered emotional, but try not to let their emotions impede their actions. They show their feelings without difficulty, unless the handwriting contains controls, such as repression or light writing. They can be sympathetic to the needs of others because of their outgoing nature.

"Four score and seven years ago our fathers brought forth on this continent, a new nation, conceived in Liberty, and dedicated to the proposition that all men are created equal.

"Now we are engaged in a great civil war, testing whether that nation or any nation so conceived and so dedicated, can long endure. We are met on a great battlefield of that war. We have come to dedicate a portion of that field, as a final resting place for those who here gave their lives that that nation might live. It is altogether fitting and proper that we should do this.

"But, in a larger sense, we can not dedicate — we can not consecrate — we can not hallow — this ground. The brave men, living and dead, who struggled here, have consecrated it, far above our poor power to add or detract. The world will little note, nor long remember what we say here, but it can never forget what they did here. It is for us, the living, rather, to be dedicated here to the unfinished work which they who fought here have thus far so nobly advanced.

(continued)

Please join me — I'm proud
be part of SFAW's campaign to
& unbelievable cruelty to the
imals in South Korea.

Help us achieve our goal of
million signatures of protest
m outraged people who refuse
ignore the suffering of animals
ywhere in the world.

You and I can and will make
difference — Please sign
e petition, and then ask your
riends and neighbors to do the
me.

The handwriting sample on the previous page belongs to
a supratype. The sample on this page was written by a
supratype plus.

If the handwriting slants very far right, the person is an
extrotype. These personalities are emotional and can be
impulsive. Sometimes they can be prone to outbursts, hysteria,
or other forms of undisciplined emotion. Both supratype plus
and extrotype personalities inwardly feel emotions very
strongly and usually show them outwardly.

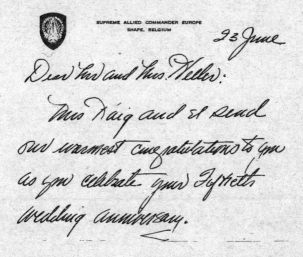

SUPREME ALLIED COMMANDER EUROPE
SHAPE, BELGIUM

23 June

Dear Mr and Mrs Weller:

*Mrs Haig and I send
our warmest congratulations to you
as you celebrate your Fiftieth
wedding anniversary.*

This handwriting sample belongs to Alexander Haig, an extrotype.

When the slant is multidirectional and doesn't fit any of the archetypes above, it is called the **varitype** slant. Varitypes tend to be flexible and are usually able to cope with any emotional situation. However, if the writing looks wild and erratic—all over the place—this usually indicates that the person is emotionally out of control in some way. Checking the rest of the handwriting is necessary to further define the problem.

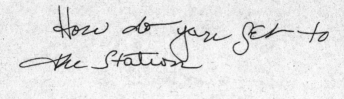

The sample on top shows the varying slant of a varitype.
The sample on the bottom is a varitype who is out of control—the slant is far too erratic.

AN EXERCISE TO DETERMINE YOUR EMOTIONAL RESPONSE

To measure your slant and determine which graphotype
you are, write a few sentences of your choosing on unlined
white paper in pencil. Take a ruler and draw a line under each
sentence and a vertical line through the middle of the page.
With a protractor, or with your eye, determine the average
angle of the writing from the baseline.

Handwriting Sample:

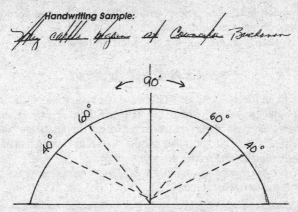

Use this method to determine your emotional response.

If your writing slants any degree to the left, you are an introtype. The farther to the left it goes, the more intense the characteristics of your introtype personality. If your slant is vertical, matching the line you drew up and down relative to the baseline, you're a supratype. If your slant is slightly to the right of the vertical, within 45 degrees, you're a supratype plus. Beyond 45 degrees, your slant puts you into the extrotype category. If your slant goes in more than one direction, you are a varitype.

To explore your emotions more fully, get out your notebook and write down your graphotype, plus a paragraph about how you see yourself emotionally. Answer these questions:

- Are you in control of your emotions?
- Are you emotionally disciplined?
- Do you allow your emotions to dominate your life?
- Are there ways you could become more emotionally mature?
- Are you satisfied with your emotional responses to situations?

Look over what you've written. If you think you need to work on your emotions, make this one of the goals you identify when working with the graphotherapy exercises.

BEGIN A PERSONAL INVENTORY

In an ideal world, we would be able to consciously choose optimal personality traits through self-directed will alone. Complete control may be unattainable, but graphotherapy can help you become receptive enough to begin communicating with yourself and others on your own terms.

As you proceed with the graphotherapy exercises, you will start to learn what it means to:

- make wiser choices for yourself
- be more conscious of your behavior than before
- be proactive and not reactive—change from passivity to taking charge of yourself
- live in the moment and realize that now is the time for action and resolution

But first, there are a few steps of preparation that you need to take before you actually start your graphotherapy program. One is to understand what motivates you.

Maslow: Master of Motivation

Over the years, psychological studies have shown repeatedly that changes in behavior are more likely to occur when individuals themselves become motivated and decide to make the change, rather than when the change is suggested to them. Why would you suddenly be motivated to change today, when you weren't yesterday or the day before? The answer may lie in the work of Abraham Maslow (1908–1970), a leading exponent of humanistic psychology.

Motivation is what causes an individual to carry out an activity. Motivation involves both conscious and unconscious drives. No single theory of motivation has been universally accepted, but Maslow's is highly respected.

Maslow developed a theory called self-actualization, a process in which an individual progresses from fulfilling basic needs such as food and sex to fulfilling the highest needs of one's human potential:

1. physiological (basic survival)
2. security and safety
3. love and feelings of belonging
4. competence, prestige, and esteem
5. self-fulfillment
6. curiosity and the need to understand

In the most developed stage of motivation, an individual is fully self-actualized and makes conscious choices. Maslow studied self-actualizers (including Abraham Lincoln, Albert Schweitzer, Albert Einstein, Thomas Jefferson, and Eleanor Roosevelt) and found these common characteristics (although not all self-actualized persons show all these characteristics):

- They perceive reality accurately and are not defensive in their perceptions of the world.
- They accept themselves, others, and nature.
- They don't lead programmed lives but are spontaneous and natural.
- They have a sense of purpose to which they dedicate their lives.
- They prefer privacy and detachment; they enjoy being alone, especially to reflect on events.
- They don't take life for granted.
- They may have had mystic or peak experiences—moments of intense activity during which the self is transcended. The individual becomes so totally involved in the experience that he or she forgets all sense of time and awareness of self.
- They express social interest.

- They have meaningful and sometimes profound interpersonal relationships.
- They have democratic characteristics and show little,
  if any, racial, religious, or social prejudice.
- They are creative, especially in managing their lives.
- They are autonomous, independent, and self-sufficient
  and can overcome the fads, whims, and pathologies of
  their culture.
- They have a philosophical sense of humor and don't
  take themselves too seriously.
- They have a high level of personal integrity.

Maslow taught that self-actualization doesn't happen
overnight and that most people are motivated by what is
important at the time. Therefore, self-actualization has to be
achieved by consciously working toward it. Some ways to
accomplish self-actualization are to:

- pay attention to your surroundings and create an effective environment to satisfy the lower needs first
- take risks—choose growth over safety and learn from
  failures
- expand into the world around yourself; especially to
  overcome cultural influences and pulls
- learn to trust yourself
- tell the truth
- recognize the need for discipline
- pay attention to your feelings
- give up your attachment to pain and fear

*You will quickly see that all of the means to self-actualiza-
tion are available in graphotherapy.* The exercises and the way
they are structured can help you become a self-actualized individual.

You Picked up This Book

This act is step one in finding the best in yourself. *You have decided you want to make changes.*

You should make an inventory of where you are now. Do this by making two lists in your notebook:

1. Traits That Work for Me
2. Traits That Weaken My Effectiveness

Be as honest and as unrelenting as you are able. For example, if you get impatient doing a particular chore, write that down. If you have a good memory, write that down. Remember, this is private, and there are no judgments. Ask one or two people you trust to write a short description of how they see you. Compare your inventory to theirs. Assess both the similarities and differences.

Set Goals and Objectives

Part of the process of defining who you are in order to know who you want to be is establishing goals and objectives. Goal setting maximizes the effectiveness of the exercises by giving you the focus to achieve what's most important to you. Your goals and objectives can be listed in your notebook under the heading "What I Want to Achieve in My Life."

As you continue to find the best in yourself, the list should change, reflecting your growth and new perceptions. As you gather and record your experiences, a new picture of yourself is going to emerge. Your current goals and objectives mirror your present conception of success, but that's going to sharpen and improve as you complete the graphotherapy exercises.

YOUR PERSONALITY IS LIKE NO OTHER

Personality is complex and unique and implies predictability about how a person will act or react under different circumstances. Because of this, it can be measured. Enduring patterns of thought, feeling, and behavior make a person unique. These characteristics don't constitute a personality, but they can help define it. There are many theories about personality, each emphasizing different aspects including its organization, development, and manifestation in behavior.

For example, psychoanalytic theory states that unconscious processes direct a great part of a person's behavior. Behaviorism, on the other hand, sees human behavior as determined largely by learned consequences—if rewarded, behavior recurs; if punished, it is less likely to recur. Heredity and environment also influence the formation of personality. Individuals differ widely because of variables that are inherited or result from conditions of pregnancy and birth and early childhood. Parental and family influences are crucial for personality development.

Some characteristics of personality can be changed. Some cannot. But all can be worked with, controlled, or redirected. This is what graphotherapy teaches you.

ANALYZE YOUR OWN HANDWRITING

You're going to undertake a simple handwriting self-analysis that will help you identify the range of personality traits you now possess. In a full graphological personality evaluation, more than three hundred individual traits are assessed and compared. The analysis you are about to take is not an in-depth study, but it will help you to better understand yourself and work more effectively with the graphotherapy exercises.

Start the analysis with a handwriting sample. On a sheet of unlined white paper, with a ballpoint pen, write whatever comes into your head. *Don't copy!* It's important that the thoughts flow directly from your mind to the page.

When you've filled up the page, use this sample to compare with the information below.

The Broad Strokes

When you look at someone's handwriting, the first thing that may strike you is the way it slants. This is the first element of the analysis, which you completed when you determined your graphotype. So next, we'll look at the pressure with which you write. Pressure indicates your energy level, your ability to cope with stress, and the sensual side of your nature. The amount of pressure applied to the paper varies from individual to individual. If you write with heavy pressure and press hard on the paper, you have these attributes:

- you are more than likely to be affected by stress
- a high energy level
- a sensual nature
- you are affected by your environment

If you write with light pressure, you have these attributes:

- the capacity to bounce back quickly from stressful situations
- relatively low vitality
- a subdued or restrained nature
- unconcern for your surroundings

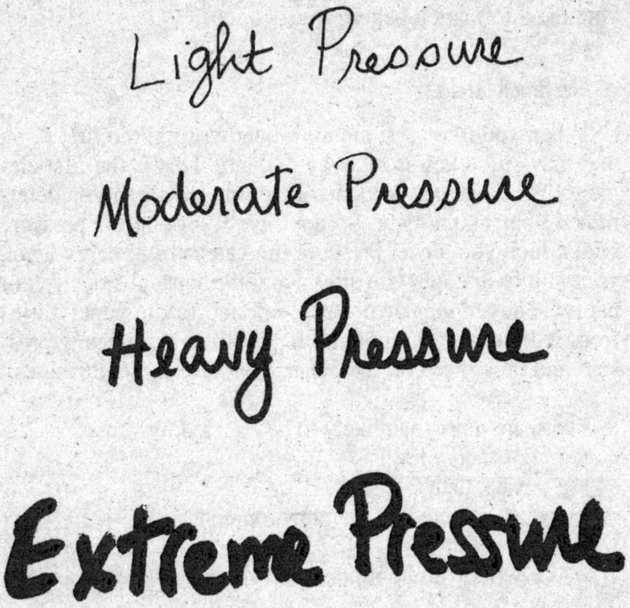

Light Pressure

Moderate Pressure

Heavy Pressure

Extreme Pressure

The top sample shows light pressure—you won't be able to feel any ridges at all in the paper. The second sample shows moderate pressure—there are slightly raised ridges on the paper. The third sample shows heavy pressure—the ridges are palpable and may feel like corduroy. The bottom sample shows extreme pressure—there may even be tears in the paper from the heavy application of the pen.

Another aspect of handwriting that graphologists examine is clarity and neatness. In school, most of us were told that neatness counts and were downgraded if our papers were illegible. In handwriting analysis, neatness doesn't count aesthetically—it takes on a different value. When people scrawl, it usually means that their thinking is faster than their ability to write the words, or they can be disorganized or lack self-discipline.

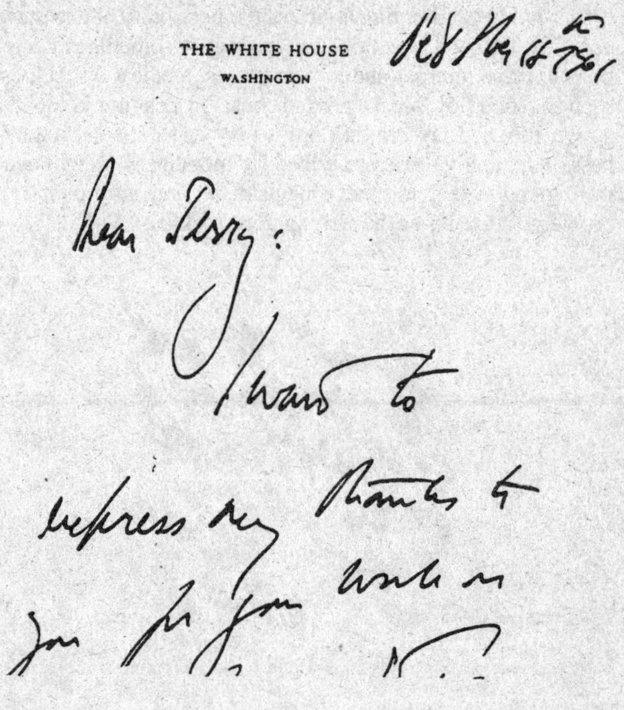

THE WHITE HOUSE
WASHINGTON

[handwritten date]

Dear Terry:

I want to

express my thanks to

you for your work on

[illegible]

This handwriting sample show scrawled writing, which indicates faster thinking than the hand can translate, or a lack of self-discipline, or disorganization. The sample is President John Kennedy's.

If the *m*'s, *n*'s, or *h*'s in scrawled writing don't have much definition, the writer thinks superficially—there's no motivation to probe below the surface.

Muddiness is another trait that sometimes occurs in handwriting. It is shown by blacked-out circle letters, primarily lowercase *e*'s. Muddiness can present a reason for serious concern. Muddy handwriting indicates the possibility of excessive appetites for food, alcohol, sex, or drugs—sometimes addictions to these things—and in some cases, medical difficulties, such as blood flow blockages and consciousness muddling. Be aware, too, that prescription drugs may cause mental muddiness, particularly those prescribed for moodiness, weight control, attention deficit, heart sluggishness, and insomnia. The problems intensify as the writing gets muddier.

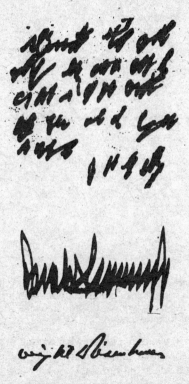

These samples of muddy writing belong to John Paul Getty, Donald Trump, and Dwight D. Eisenhower, respectively.

Rhythm is another significant trait. It's an evaluated trait, meaning that it is measured in degrees, just as pressure is. The presence of rhythm is characterized by the fluid motion of the pen across the page. If you write with a consistent, smooth flow that never seems to break stride, you've got rhythm. Generally, rhythm is one indication of how you approach situations and how you function daily. The specific attributes of rhythmic writing are:

- constancy of behavior
- a preference for keeping situations on an even keel
- desire for some degree of routine in life
- dislike of the routine being disturbed

Lack of rhythm can indicate:

- versatility
- adaptability
- erratic behavior

> it is he that hath made us,
> and not we ourselves; we are
> his people, and the sheep of
> his pasture. Enter into his
> gates with thanksgiving, and
> into his courts with praise:
> be thankful unto him, and
> bless his name. For the Lord
> is good; his mercy is ever-
> lasting; and his truth endureth
> to all generations. ———

> ... many to you, Beginning with
> said that we would serve me

The top sample shows handwriting with rhythm—notice that it is beautiful and flowing. By contrast, the handwriting below it has no rhythm—it appears jerky and awkward.

Another general element that a graphologist looks at is spacing—the area left between letters, words, and lines and the area left for margins (the borders surrounding the writing). The use of space is an evaluated trait, and generally, the following applies:

- The width of the margins indicates generosity or frugality.
- The spacing between words, letters, and lines shows conservatism or unconventionality.

greetings!
This is just to let you
know I'll be going to
the mall tomorrow, so
if you want to come
with me let me
know ASAP.
Thanks!

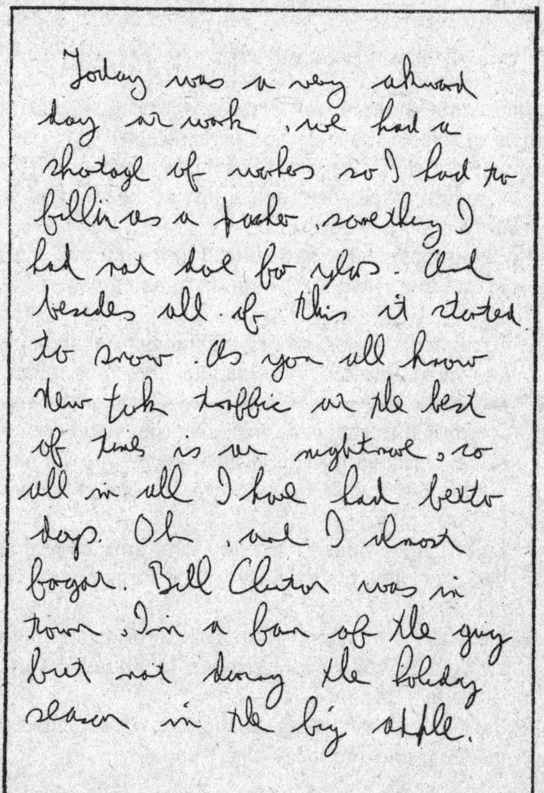

> Today was a very awkward day at work, we had a shotage of workes so I had to fill in as a packer, something I had not done for yers. And besides all of this it started to snow. As you all know New York traffic at the best of times is a nightmare, so all in all I have had better days. Oh, and I almost forgot. Bill Clinton was in town. I'm a fan of the guy but not during the holiday season in the big apple.

The left sample shows much space left between sentences and in the margins, indicating an extravagant individual. The illustration above shows a certain frugality—the writer runs each sentence fully from the left to the right margin. However, there is space at the top and bottom margin, as well as in the other elements of the writing, which greatly mitigates any tendency toward conservatism. These samples show why spacing is an evaluated trait; there are various ways space can be used.

UNDERSTAND YOUR THINKING PATTERNS

Like slant (emotional responsiveness), another fundamental element of your personality that is represented in handwriting is the way you think, referred to as thinking patterns. Thinking patterns represent the speed and agility of the mind, as well as how information is processed.

Thinking patterns are symbolized in the way we make our *m*'s, *n*'s, and *h*'s. There are five basic thinking patterns:

1. Analytical thinkers size up situations from all angles, shown by inverted V formations seen most often in *m*'s and *n*'s.
2. Intuitional thinkers can make decisions without conscious reasoning. This ability speeds up all other thinking patterns. It is shown by breaks between letters.
3. Investigative thinkers like to search for answers and get information, shown by wedge formations in *m*'s and *n*'s.
4. Methodical thinkers mull over information before arriving at conclusions, shown by rounded formations in *m*'s and *n*'s.
5. Quick thinkers' minds are lightning fast, shown by needle points primarily in *m*'s and *n*'s.

Here are illustrations of the various kinds of thinking patterns.

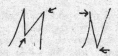

Analytical: V-shaped formations, primarily in the *m*'s and *n*'s. Such minds can weigh and evaluate data and come to conclusions.

myself and to discuss

Intuitive: Breaks between the letters in a word. Intuition helps bridge the gaps in data to achieve conclusions. Intuition speeds up methodical/logical thinking, with surprisingly good results.

My Main idea is to Mellow out.

Investigative: Wedge or mountaintop formations in *m*'s and *n*'s and other letters. These writers will research on their own for data and retrieve it. Usually they can also analyze.

m   n

Methodical (Logical): Rounded tops on *m*'s and *n*'s. All data must be in order, precise methods of categorization and comparison take place, and one step must follow another in sequence. This can take a relatively long time. Combined with an analytical mind, answers may seem excruciatingly slow in coming. This person does not work well on deadline.

Many minor episodes of murder.

Quick/comprehensive: Needle point tops on *m*'s and *n*'s. Quick, visually adapted mind. Learns and thinks faster than most.

Thinking patterns don't necessarily indicate intelligence level. It is a grave mistake to assume that a methodical thinker is any less intelligent than a person who has the ability to process information faster. The methodical thinker reflects more than the quick thinker does, even though he or she may be evenly matched in comprehension and other mental attributes.

A MINIGLOSSARY OF TRAITS

Graphology is a highly structured, multifaceted discipline. At this point, you can't analyze your handwriting in depth, but you don't need to. I've developed this miniglossary to give you the essential, basic information for your self-analysis. Compare your handwriting to the symbols on the chart below. In analyzing your own handwriting, you will see where both strengths and weaknesses lie. Do not become overly concerned about any perceived weaknesses—it's common to give weaknesses more attention than they deserve. While it's important to acknowledge that we have traits that hold us back, it's equally important not to dwell on them or give them undue importance.

Use this handwriting self-analysis to prioritize the graphotherapy exercises that follow. When you complete all the exercises in *Rewrite Your Life*, you should repeat this self-evaluation by writing out a new page and comparing it to the chart and your original self-analysis.

Low goals: low *t* bar on stem

Practical goals: *t* bar in middle of stem

High goals: *t* bar high on stem

Dreamer or visionary: *t* bar floats above stem

Enthusiasm: sweeping *t* bar

Procrastination: bar to left of stem only

Temper: bar to right of stem only

t   yes I can

Optimistic: bar slants up and writing slants up

no I can't

Pessimistic: writing slants down

t

Sarcastic: arrow-shaped bar

t

Shallow in purpose: basin-shaped bar

t

Self-control: umbrella-shaped bar

t

Stubborn: tentlike stem

Dignity: retraced stem

Sensitivity to criticism: looped *t* or *d* stem

Independence: short *t* stem

Pride: stem is twice the size of lowercase letters

Vanity: stem is three times the size of lowercase letters

i

Detail orientation: well-placed "*i*" dot

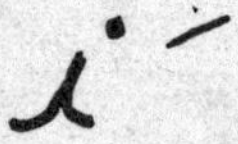

i

Some detail orientation: traveling "*i*" dot

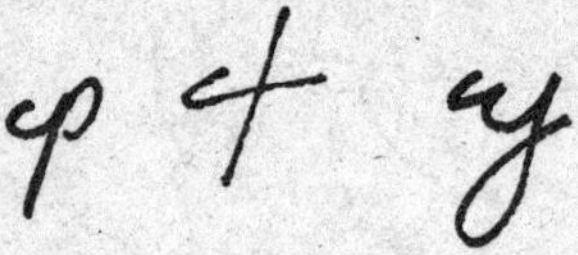

φ φ y

Acquisitive: initial hook at beginning of a letter

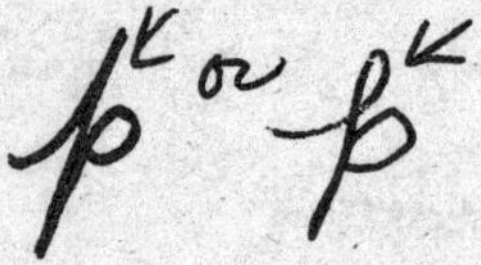

p or p

Argumentative: high *p* stem

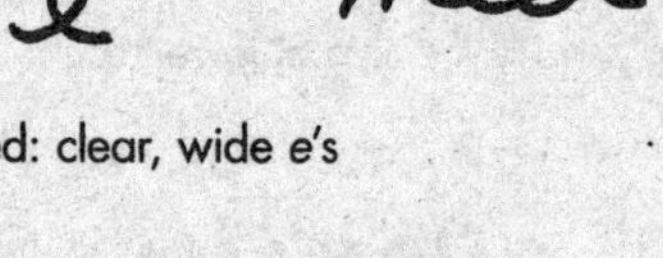

e   meet

Broad-minded: clear, wide *e*'s

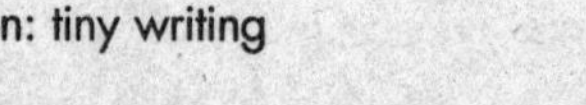

concentration

Concentration: tiny writing

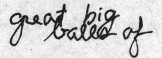

great big balls of

Confusion: letters and words overlap

when the bill was passed

Conservative: compressed letters

yes great zip jolly

Creative/imaginative: full lower loops on *g*'s, *y*'s, *j*'s, and *z*'s

R

Defiant: big *k* buckle

this

Desires attention: final stroke that is long and partially curved backward

man

Diplomatic: tapering *m*'s and *n*'s

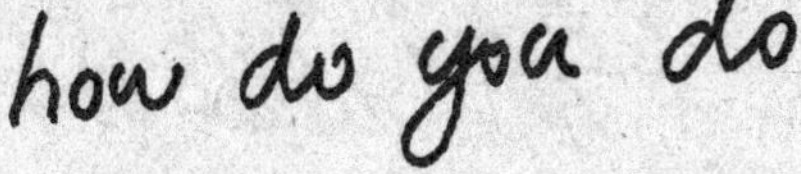

how do you do

Direct: no initial strokes

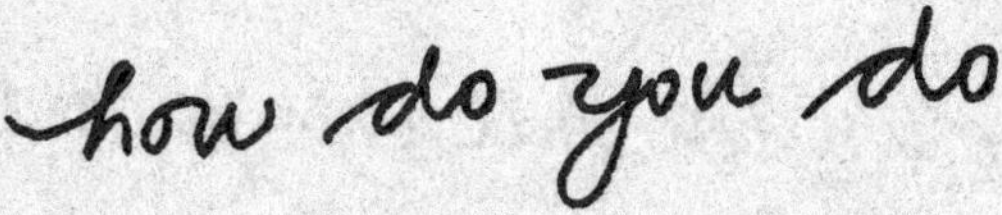

how do you do

Indirect: approach strokes (at beginning of letters)

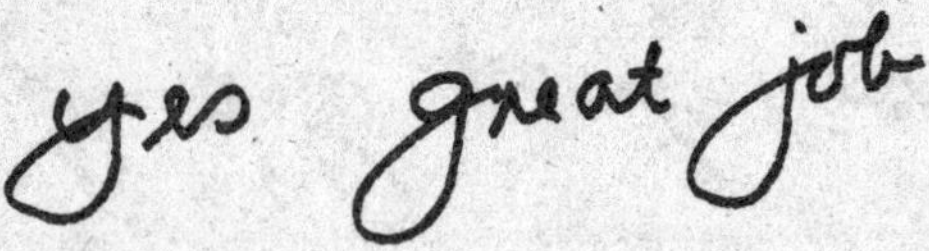

yes great job

Exaggeration: overblown lower loops

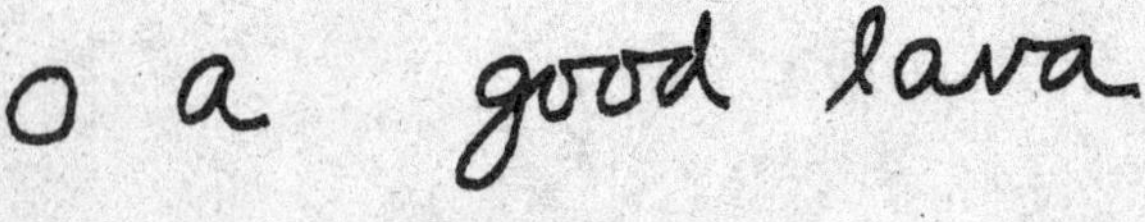

o a good lava

Frank, honest: clear, open o's and a's

way yes

Generosity: long final strokes and wide spacing between letter combinations

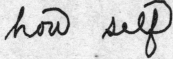

Guilt: final stroke reverses direction and veers to the left

great

Initiative: breakaway final *t* stroke

intuition

Intuition: breaks between letters

money no

Jealousy: small loops at the beginning of *m*'s and *n*'s

i j

Loyalty: round "*i*" or *j* dot

Organizational ability: top and bottom of lowercase *f* equally balanced

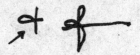

Persistence: tie strokes

Philosophic: full upper loops on *h*'s, *b*'s, and *l*'s

Precision: retraced *p* stem

Resentment: inflexible, rigid approach stroke

Secrecy: loop on right side of *o*'s or *a*'s

Self-deceit: loop on left side of o's or a's

Self-confident: large capital letters

Self-conscious: exaggerated *n* hump or second *m* hump

Self-reliance: underlined signature

Sense of humor: initial flourish on *m*'s or *n*'s

a o

Talkative: *a*'s and *o*'s open at the top

Caw *d* *m*

Tenacity: hook at the end of a word

UNDERSTANDING COMPATIBILITY

Of course you don't exist in a vacuum, and you're constantly interacting with other human beings. Handwriting analysis is very useful in helping you understand how you will get along with others. Compatibility assessments are especially important for close personal relationships and for business partnerships and team building.

Many traits can be compared, but those that are most important are slant/emotional response, stress level, and thinking patterns, for these are core traits that do not change. For example, can a person with a low tolerance for stress work well with a person who has a high tolerance for stress? Can a boss who thinks with lightning quick speed work well with individuals who must mull their thoughts first? Can a person with a far right slant find happiness with a person who has a left slant? These are some of the questions a compatibility analysis seeks to answer in graphology.

Of course, all of the exercises in *Rewrite Your Life* are designed to promote self-awareness, and controls and modifications can be developed for the core traits that don't change. People who are seemingly incompatible, yet who are willing to work on building a great relationship can do so through graphotherapy.

4
EXERCISE PREPARATION

IF YOU PUT A THOUGHT IN SOMEONE'S MIND, WHERE DOES IT go? I've often wondered about this question. I'm going to be putting many thoughts in your mind, which I hope will become seeds for growth.

The graphotherapy exercises are designed so that you can begin to put the various aspects of your life into perspective and become more aware of your potentials. You have the ability not only to understand the nature of personal success but also to let nothing stop you from attaining the level of achievement that's comfortable and appropriate for you.

UNDERSTAND THE PURPOSE OF THE SEED THOUGHTS

Almost every graphotherapy handwriting exercise contains a core message integral to the exercise. These thoughts flow from pen to hand to brain, are internalized, and eventually become integrated into new belief patterns. For example, an exercise about persistence might include the phrase: I will stick with what I'm doing until it's finished. This sentence defines the nature of persistence, and as you write it out, it starts to redefine or to enhance your belief(s) about persistence. The graphotherapy exercises all have the same primary objective: to promote mental and emotional well-being. Each, of course, has a specific objective, linked to the trait it's addressing (such as persistence or determination or sense of humor).

PLANTING SEEDS—CHANGING BEHAVIOR

Graphotherapy works with behavior principles in that you can change your behavior by monitoring it. You can extinguish nonproductive behaviors and reinforce productive ones by using the seed thoughts to program new ideas about the way you behave. In this respect, graphotherapy is like cognitive behavior modification, which is a marriage between two traditional therapies: cognitive therapy and behavior modification therapy.

Cognition is the process by which we can know; it includes memory, perception, attention, reasoning, imagining, thinking, judgment, and speech. In cognitive psychology, the emphasis is on information handling. The theory of cognitive consistency states that our beliefs and actions are logically consistent with one another. When dissonance (the lack of such consistency) arises, we automatically (and unconsciously) try to restore consistency by changing our behavior, beliefs, or perceptions. The aim of cognitive therapy, then, is to get rid of dissonance and unproductive behaviors in a conscious mode and to replace unproductive behaviors with productive ones. The core of the therapy deals with self-perception and personal beliefs and creating new realities of being. These are some of the basic cognitive concepts:

- You determine your own life.
- Your thoughts shape your behavior.
- Problems are problems of consciousness.
- It is not necessary to know the cause of a problem in order to solve it.
- Behavior is motivated by a desire to solve problems, complete tasks, or reach goals.

- Perceptions, emotions, goals, and behavior exert reciprocal influences on each other.

These concepts are very much a part of graphotherapy.

Behavior modification principles are based on the assumption that behaviors can be changed by monitoring and conditioning them. The aim of behavior modification is to acquire self-control, extinguish nonproductive behaviors, and reinforce productive ones through various methods including desensitization, aversion therapy, and biofeedback.

In graphotherapy, behavior change is accomplished in the biofeedback mode, by the use of repetitive handwriting exercises and by keeping logs and records of successes.

CREATE YOUR ENVIRONMENT AND ASSEMBLE YOUR MATERIALS

To work effectively with the graphotherapy exercises, you need to create a conducive environment and gather some simple materials. You already have your notebook. In addition, you need:

- ballpoint pens
- number-2 pencils
- lined and unlined 8½ x 11 paper
- classical/soothing music
- contemporary/upbeat music
- a comfortable chair
- a desk or table to lean on comfortably
- a good lamp or abundance of natural light
- a quiet location with good ventilation

You're now ready to start the exercises!

APPROACH EACH EXERCISE IN FIVE STEPS

This is how every graphotherapy exercise should be approached:

1. Allot fifteen minutes (at least) every day to the exercises. Try to do them at the same time every day; this strengthens commitment to positive change and reinforces the learning curve.
2. Ideally, schedule your exercises in the morning and/or evening, with music to lead in or accompany: ten to fifteen minutes of upbeat music in the morning; ten minutes of calming music in the evening.
3. Before you begin, take three deep breaths with your eyes closed.
4. Sit up tall, with your feet firmly on the floor, and get comfortable.
5. Plant in your mind what it is you want to accomplish; concentrate on the focused thought.

Every time you do an exercise, you'll also write a cover sheet containing these data:

- name of the exercise
- date
- time of day
- how you felt before, during and after the exercise
- noteworthy events in your life today

Sign each sheet after you fill it in.

Keeping this log is extremely important, because as you start doing the exercises and begin to see results, the log will show you how you got the results. The log not only helps you track your successes but also lets you pinpoint areas that may need more work. The log also serves as a diary for you.

GRAPHOTHERAPY LOG

Name of exercise _____

Date_____

Time_____

NOTEWORTHY EVENTS TODAY

MY GOAL(S)

FEELINGS

Before exercise:

During exercise:

After exercise:

_____
                                                        (Signed)

START THE WORK!

The pages that follow contain relaxation exercises, followed by graphotherapy exercises. The sequence of the graphotherapy exercises is important *because each one helps you build the strengths you need to successfully work with the next.* However, if you believe you need to work on any exercise out of sequence, feel free to do so. Depending on your own personality and your needs, you may want to choose specific graphotherapy exercises according to your personal inventory and goals and objectives list. In this case, work first on the traits you feel you need to deal with most. You can always go back or forward or repeat any exercise as you choose. *However, I strongly recommend that you eventually work on all of the exercises given in this book.* When you complete all the exercises, you'll find that the result—the sum—is greater than the parts.

Work at your own pace, selecting the number and frequency of the exercises you want to do. Note that all the exercises, unless otherwise indicated, are done on plain, white, unlined sheets with a ballpoint pen. Otherwise, follow the specific directions for each.

Always record your thoughts and reactions to each exercise in your notebook after you complete them.

RELAXATION

The relaxation exercises are given first because they MUST be done every time you do a graphotherapy exercise. A relaxed state is required before starting your graphotherapy session.

Anxiety—apprehension, worry, dread, uneasiness—is a type of mental discomfort we've all felt at one time or another. Anxiety is the most common psychological disorder in the United States, affecting two to four percent of the population. Anxiety may be relatively mild, be a feature of panic attacks, or be chronic and generalized. Physical symptoms can include muscle tension, sweaty palms, upset stomach, shortness of breath, feelings of faintness, and a pounding heart. The cause of anxiety is debatable, although evidence suggests that anxiety runs in families.

Some theorists believe that anxiety is learned when innate fears become associated with previously neutral objects or events. For example, an infant frightened by a loud noise while playing with a toy may become anxious just at the sight of the toy. Other theorists stress the importance of imitative behavior and the development of particular thought patterns. A common feature is that the individual fears he or she won't be able to master future events.

Traditionally, drugs, psychotherapy, behavior modification, and relaxation training, alone or in combination, are used in treating anxiety. *In graphotherapy, the relaxation exercises can greatly help to calm anxieties, especially mild ones.* These exercises can also be done any time you feel the need to reduce stress or tension, or simply increase your feelings of well-being.

Your mind and body absorb information best when you are loose and at ease. There are many relaxation exercises in graphotherapy. All of them, when practiced regularly, will help:

- improve your rhythm
- release tension
- promote stability
- create balance and harmony

Any of the relaxation exercises can be done at any time to great advantage, but they are especially effective:

- in the evening before bed
- whenever you feel stressed, either at home or in the office, take fifteen minutes out of your schedule to do them
- on the phone instead of doodling
- before you begin any graphotherapy exercise

When you do the relaxation exercises, try to be as rhythmic and as graceful as possible. Create a dance with your
hand and pen. Also, remember when you were a very young
child and how you probably enjoyed scribbling with unfet-
tered abandon. It's this free and fluid quality you want to
achieve when you work with these exercises.

Choose a different relaxation exercise each day. If you
have a preferred relaxation exercise, do it daily, along with
a second relaxation exercise that you vary each day.

Fill up at least a page. Where applicable, don't lift your
pen off the page until the end of a line. The motion of your
hand should be a continuous, steady flow, line for line, down
the entire page.

Don't forget the two relaxation exercises on pages 24–26.

These exercises look so elementary and simple on paper
that you wonder if you are back in kindergarten. Don't be
deceived by their apparent simplicity. Each exercise requires
concentration, fluidity, and precision to be executed prop-
erly. Of course, the more you do them, the easier they
become, and you will readily see—and feel—their benefits
as time goes on.

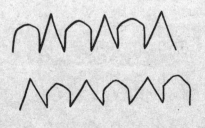

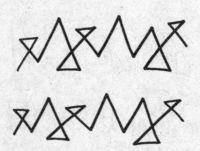

lelelelelelelelelel
lelelelelelelelelel
lelelelelelelelelel

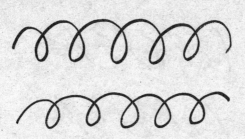

VISUALIZATION

I often use visualizations in conjunction with graphotherapy exercises. Visualizations are like watching a scene unfold on the TV screen of the mind. Perhaps you've seen athletes running visualizations prior to participating in sporting events. A bobsledder, for example, closes his eyes and sees the run of the sled down the entire track, curve by curve. His eyes closed, his hands and body move along with his inner vision, seeing the run in his mind's eye in its most perfect form from start to finish. First the bobsledder experiences the event in his mind; all that remains is to actualize the vision by executing it as conceived.

Visualizations are not just for athletes. They are a powerful mental technique that can help anyone reinforce anything that needs to be learned or accomplished. In my practice I guide clients through visualizations as part of graphotherapy—they help strengthen the entire process. If you were sitting in my office, I would tailor the visualizations to your individual needs, but since this is not the case, we'll try this visualization using this technique:

Read the following paragraph. Then put the book aside, get comfortable, close your eyes, and picture the scene described with as much detail as possible:

You have a report that is due soon and is important to your job. You feel anxious about completing it successfully. Picture yourself sitting down at your desk full of confidence and creative ideas. You make yourself comfortable, and then you attack. You pick up your pen or place your fingers on the keyboard of your computer and begin to write. You find the thoughts coming to you with utter ease, almost faster than you can record them. You find that you are on a roll and that the outside world fades away as you complete your task. Time has no meaning as you fly through your work. Finally you have finished in what seems like a mere instant. The report is done. You feel satisfied and proud of your accomplishment. What's more, you know that the work you've done is excellent and will be well received by your boss. Your persistence has paid off. You feel very good about yourself and what you have done.

How does this visualization make you feel? Run it through your head a second time, and a third. Do you still feel the same way about it? Record all of these thoughts in your notebook. Compare the differences, if there are any, and examine why you feel differently after each visualization, if you do. If you don't feel any difference, explore why you think that is the case.

The visualization you have just done is one of any number of positive tapes you can play in your head in conjunction with graphotherapy.

Develop your own visualizations.

Here are some other themes you can use:

- See yourself as you are now. Then change the picture to a desired self-image. See yourself as you'd like to be. Learn to stand in awe of yourself.
- Visualize being responsible. See yourself in charge of situations that are uncomfortable for you, partic-

ularly those that happen over the course of a typical day. Self-trust is the first secret of success.

- Think about the areas of harmony and disharmony in your life. Think about how your attitudes and beliefs contribute to these areas. Now focus on a current event in your life that you feel is not in harmony. Visualize a change in attitude or belief and see yourself feeling inner peace and well-being.
- See yourself in various professions, doing different jobs. Thoroughly explore the ones that give you the greatest satisfaction.

Whenever you do a visualization, keep in mind that you can change the picture as you desire. Don't hesitate to do so. Examine all the possibilities of your potential self. Go around the dials. Stay tuned to the images that appeal most to you.

Think about your strongest traits and always reinforce them. In your visualizations, as in your planning, set goals that meet your potentials. Always see yourself doing what you want to do and accomplishing what you want to accomplish. Tear down all barriers to success. You can do anything you want to on the TV screen of your mind. Be sure to write down how you feel about these experiences. Be as descriptive as possible.

AFFIRMATION

Along with visualizations, I use affirmations in graphotherapy. Affirmations are statements of belief that help us reinforce all the positive work we're striving toward. These are sayings that can be spoken aloud, expressed privately as thoughts, or written out. No matter what method of affirmation you choose, you should affirm at least once a day, preferably when you are doing your exercises. If you are writing your affirmations, be sure to write the date and the time and sign your pages. Here are a few sample affirmations:

- I am now doing what enhances my potential and will allow me to advance.
- I am releasing my energies and opening up my mind in order to accomplish my goals.
- I have confidence in my ability to succeed in whatever I desire.
- I learn from my feelings and experiences.
- I am looking to the left and right instead of straight ahead.

Practice creating your own affirmations as you do the work of graphotherapy. The only rule is to be positive and optimistic.

ALERTNESS

Alertness is the state of being keenly aware, attentive, and vigilant. In an alert state you possess mental vitality and have the potential to increase the performance of your mind and body. Hence, the result of being alert has both psychological and physical consequences. Many performance lapses arise from distractions.

Alertness places you in a state of readiness and focus. This in turn allows action. Without alertness you can become inattentive and unaware and therefore unable to accomplish or act. For example, research has shown that athletes who reach the level of Olympic competition are more alert than their unsuccessful colleagues because they do more mental practice in preparing for tryouts. This mental practice, which includes mental rehearsal and visualization, teaches the brain and body to be in a state of readiness. The techniques add a dynamic element to the learning process and open up new possibilities of potential because the brain uses the information as a model for performance. By reconstructing external events in the mind, the brain is programmed to be alert.

The following drawings will increase your capacity for alertness, help stimulate your left and right brains, and help you focus and eliminate hesitation and distraction while doing the graphotherapy exercises. Copy at least one page of these drawings a day.

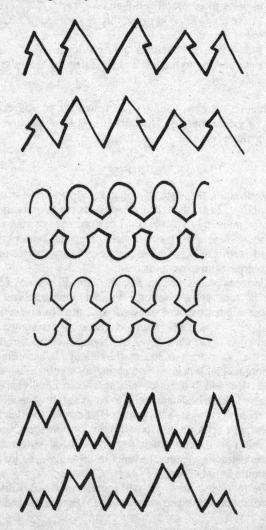

5
RECEPTIVITY EXERCISES

THIS CHAPTER BEGINS THE SERIES OF GRAPHOTHERAPY EXER-
cises based on traits you'll be strengthening. There are five
groups in total.

This first group contains three exercises that prime you
and open you up for all of the subsequent exercises. The first
exercise helps you *concentrate*; the second helps develop
your *intuitive* capacity, so that you are working on a higher
level than just your five senses; and the third allows you to
be *open-minded* and receptive to the entire process.

CONCENTRATION

Concentration is your ability to work without letting outside influences interfere. It is the ability to fix your attention
on a task by keeping distracting thoughts away. Concentration
is not an inborn ability but must be learned and developed like
any other skill. Developing an ability to concentrate involves
establishing some level of concentration, increasing that level,
and developing a concentration habit.

To accomplish this objective, become aware of the external distractions around you and separate yourself from them.
Likewise be aware of internal distractions (such as thoughts,

hunger, tiredness) and control them. Successful concentration also depends on preparedness, on planning to attend to or accomplish the task at hand. For example, you might plan to divide a complex task into manageable parts, or plan breaks. It is also helpful to be as actively involved as possible in what you are doing (for example, making notes or underlining material you are reading, or reading aloud) and to establish a pattern for concentrating, such as a regular place or time to do your work.

Concentration is an act of will, which when present in a marked degree affects all other traits shown in the writing. For example, if you are good with details, it is very beneficial for you to use your skills of concentration, as the trait will be several times stronger. The result of good concentration is efficiency and productivity—you get more done. Effective concentration also helps you improve your memory and attain clarity in your thinking. Clarity is one of the most significant traits we found in the handwriting of members of the Young Presidents Organization. We analyzed 425 handwritings through our computerized program, and clarity was one of the highest-rated traits. Strengthening the will through concentration improves the capacity for self-discipline.

In handwriting, the ability to concentrate is shown in very small handwriting.

The very small writing in this sample shows that this individual has the ability to concentrate.

On day one, start by writing the following sentence with exaggerated letter size on lined paper (lined paper lends a structure):

I focus my attention completely.

Then write the words a little smaller.

I focus my attention completely.
I focus my attention completely.
I focus my attention completely.
I focus my attention completely.
I focus my attention completely.
I focus my attention completely.
I focus my attention completely.
I focus my attention completely.
I focus my attention completely.
I focus my attention completely.
I focus my attention completely.
I focus my attention completely.
I focus my attention completely.
I focus my attention completely.
I focus my attention completely.
I focus my attention completely.

The concentration vortex is a very powerful tool for developing concentration ability. It is done on days two and three of the concentration exercise.

On day two, on lined paper, write the sentence over and over, beginning very large and diminishing the size each time you write it.

On day three, still on lined paper, write the sentence over and over as small as you can, no matter how uncomfortable it feels.

On day four, switch to unlined paper and write a sentence of your choosing over and over again, filling up one page, as tiny as you can.

In addition, on every day of the exercise, copy these drawings, making them smaller and smaller down the page until they are as small as you can draw them, yet still retain their form.

Copying these two drawings will help you develop concentration. Start with the size shown here and reduce
the size down the page until you can draw the form no
smaller.

The goal of the exercise is to feel the sensations of concentration and self-discipline. Your handwriting won't actually change and become smaller, but you will be training yourself to develop the skill of concentration. You will see exactly what it feels like to take extra time focusing in on your tasks. There aren't any threatening elements, and you will achieve a new discipline that can be most useful.

Susan Styles is a woman with normally large handwriting. Susan's poor concentration skills were due to the fact that she never developed effective study habits as a student. In conversation, she bounced from topic to topic without ever fully completing her thoughts on any one subject. Susan sought graphotherapy because her job required completion of many different tasks, and her lack of concentration was beginning to interfere with her productivity. She found herself getting scattered in her thinking, and she apparently wasn't effective in any one task. Her last performance review was not good, and she was issued a warning.

In the beginning, Susan did not have an easy time with the concentration exercise. Practicing it was arduous for her, and she became moody and more and more irritable the smaller she had to write. In time, however, as she developed her skills and her motivation to keep her job became stronger, Susan found the exercise easier to accomplish. Her handwriting did not become appreciably smaller, but Susan did learn to handle the discipline required by her job. Whenever her energy carried her away, she returned to this exercise to improve her focus and rid herself of scattered thinking. Susan wrote me a letter saying that she realized for the first time in her life that she had options.

Dear Lu
Come as you are!
See you tomorrow!

Susan's handwriting is very large, indicating that she often finds it very difficult to concentrate.

INTUITION

Intuition is one of the most valuable traits of all to possess. It can fill up your world because intuition is the quality that allows you to be receptive. Intuition can be broadly defined as a sense of knowing without apparent or seeming explanation of where the information came from. The cognition may seem independent of experience or reason, a kind of sixth sense.

Intuitive knowledge is generally regarded as an inherent quality of the mind. In graphology, intuition is considered a thinking pattern that has the capacity to speed up the others (see page 56). The concept of intuition arose from the mathematical idea of an axiom (a self-evident proposition that requires no proof) and the mystical idea of revelation (truth that surpasses the power of the intellect).

Intuition is a profound part of human nature and human experience. The difficulty is that many of us simply don't use this faculty. But it is deeply important that we do so. Having well-developed intuitive skills can help you to "sense out" new situations and make determinations using your instincts when there isn't time to analyze and weigh your data, or when there aren't any data. Moreover, developing intuition gives you a head start by making you aware of the nature of problems or circumstances at hand—you can sense the moods and feelings of others. Due to its nature, intuition can provide you with a great social and business advantage.

In handwriting, intuition is seen in breaks between letters within words. These breaks can occur anywhere and are not always represented by printed letters. There can be one break or several within a word. Sometimes people cover up their own intuitive ability because they are afraid of it. This is seen where the gaps are filled in or retraced.

The upper handwriting sample shows intuition—notice the breaks between letter formations. The sample on the bottom shows that the writer has intuition but doesn't trust this capacity within herself. You can see how the writer has gone back over the words and has covered up the trait by artificially connecting the breaks.

THE VICE PRESIDENT'S HOUSE
WASHINGTON, D.C. 20501

are doing--for the children and the
community!

With best wishes,

Sincerely, + warmly —

Barbara Bush

I don't know what you're doing
at Emory - but you're certainly
doing it well!

I told my husband about
your wonderful program!

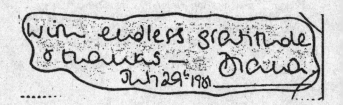

With endless gratitude
& thanks — Diana
July 29th 1981

The handwritings of Barbara Bush and Princess Diana
show a great deal of intuition.

Paula Duffy is an actress. Her reason for seeking counseling was unrelated to her profession, but I couldn't help noticing the lack of intuition in her handwriting and wondered how this might affect her acting. I knew that Paula was talented and worked on her skills in acting classes, but it seemed to me that she could be much better in her craft if she would only learn to develop her intuition. Paula agreed. She couldn't deny that this trait could benefit her tremendously, not only as an actress but in all areas of her life. We added intuition to the roster of traits she would work on. To say that a higher degree of intuition changed Paula's life is an understatement. Honing this skill not only opened up her acting ability but also provided many extra advantages. For one thing, when she auditioned, competing with literally a hundred or more actors for one job, her heightened intuition led her to make the best choices possible. Paula got more roles than she'd ever been able to get before, and her reputation as an actress increased and spread throughout the theater community.

There were other benefits too: Her self-esteem increased, which helped her tackle some of the issues she originally came to me about.

This agreement is satisfactory and I think we can make a deal that w

Recently I saw a show on Broadway that was very innovative and fresh.

The top sample is Paula's former handwriting, showing no intuitive sense. Later samples, such as the one below, show the intuition that Paula worked to develop.

Susan Parker, unlike Paula Duffy, had intuitive skills, but she tried to cover them up. She hadn't yet learned that if you want to make the right choices for yourself in life, it's essential that you allow your intuition to be your guide. Susan was in her mid-thirties, unmarried, and terribly unhappy that she couldn't find Mr. Right. In fact, to her it seemed that all the men she'd dated had turned out to be unsatisfactory in one way or another.

What was clear to me on examining Susan's handwriting was that she tried to cover up the most important trait that anyone can have in life: intuition. This she did because of fear. She simply didn't trust herself, and so she kept making the wrong personal choices. Susan's graphotherapy consisted largely of developing her intuition, both through the handwriting exercises and socialization tasks, such as the one we will get to shortly. Eventually, she became unstuck and began to trust herself. Her handwriting showed that she no longer needed to cover up the intuition trait. Eventually, Susan met a man who was, unlike his predecessors, supportive and an equal partner in their relationship. This relationship lasted for several years until it played itself out—both partners realized that although they were companionable, there was no future for them as a couple. They parted amicably and keep in touch from time to time. Susan began dating again, still looking for Mr. Right, now with the ability to make better choices in that direction than she ever possessed before.

Susan's writing shows how she covered up her trait of intuition. She never realized that she was doing it until it was pointed out to her in graphotherapy.

To develop your intuition, do this exercise for at least three days—and up to ten if you choose. Start with one or two relaxation exercises of your choice.

Next, fill up half of a page with this sentence:

Intuition opens new horizons.

As you write the sentence, make at least one break between letters in each word. Now, from the middle to the bottom of the page, put in two breaks per word. This may look like printing to you, but it's not. Yours are scripted letters that are sometimes unconnected, not block-letter printing, which has no natural ligatures.

Intuition opens new horizons

Intuition opens new horizons

Intuition opens new horizons

Intuition opens new horizons

Intuition opens new horizons

Practice the intuition exercise so that the writing begins in your regular script and evolves to look almost like printing.

As you repeat the exercise, try putting even more breaks in the words. Next, copy these symbols, filling up at least one page with each. Keep the rhythm steady.

These symbols will help you develop intuition. Fill up at least a page with each symbol.

If you are in a position to meet new people, either personally or in a business context, practice the trait of intuition by trying to sense people out. Intuit what they do for a living, what job positions they hold, their interests and hobbies, and so on.

OPEN-MINDEDNESS

To have an open mind is to be receptive in all ways—intellectually, emotionally, and spiritually. Open-mindedness is the means by which individuals as well as societies and entire cultures may thrive and grow. Perhaps the most acute way to drive home this point is to list what can happen when there is no capacity to be open-minded. In other words, when an individual, society, or culture is closed-minded the following can occur:

- prejudice and bigotry
- stereotyping
- censorship
- denial of civil rights
- repression
- subjugation
- stagnancy

Rigid thinking is the product of closed-mindedness. It is the tendency to perceive life as a series of either/or alternatives. For example, events are either right or wrong, fair or unfair, black or white. There are often many things that "should," "must," or "can't" be done by oneself or others. Hence, since there are "correct" ways to do things, rigid rules come into being. If the rules aren't adhered to, the consequences may be upsetting.

By contrast, open-mindedness has at its root the development of personal and social freedom and progress. Democracy, for example, cannot exist where there is no open-mindedness. On an individual level, open-mindedness allows the flexible and adaptive change fundamental to self-awareness and personal reform.

By its nature, open-mindedness opposes restraints. Without it, individuals would never be able to better their position in the social order, express themselves freely, share opinions, worship as they see fit, marry whomever they wish, and so on. In other words, the facility to have an open mind cuts across all dimensions of life. Personal, social, political, and economic opportunities for self-expression would not be possible without an open mind. Open-mindedness is the quality that removes obstacles to individual choice. All personal freedoms evolve from the open-mindedness of government, and conversely, the governance of the people is determined by the open-mindedness of the individuals who participate in it. If the tone is set from the top, the ideals of open-mindedness flow into the national consciousness.

On a strictly intimate, personal level, broadening one's mind and being responsive to new ideas is not only an asset but also a necessity if you want to succeed in life. Open-mindedness aids in personal relationships by providing a tolerant attitude toward the beliefs and lifestyles of others. Developing it can also free you from traditional constraints and provide you with the desire to explore new avenues of opportunity. Open-mindedness is the key to all that is new and/or possible. Without it, no one would be able, in the words of *Star Trek*, to "explore strange new worlds and seek out new life and new civilizations—to boldly go where no one has gone before."

Open-mindedness is shown in handwriting by open loops in the lowercase *e*. Conversely, narrow-mindedness is indicated by compressed *e*'s.

Have you ever been frustrated by a friend or family member who won't try new kinds of foods or go to the opera or ballet or do anything he or she hasn't done before? Next time you are confronted with this situation, look at that person's handwriting. Examine it for compressed *e*'s.

Surprisingly, narrow-mindedness is often seen in the handwriting of business executives. Many of them are not receptive to graphotherapy because of this trait.

here's my handwriting
sample for you
to analyse so that you can
look into it & analyse

The changes that have come since
I last saw you have been many - and

The top sample shows a writer who is open-minded. The bottom sample, with its compressed *e*'s, shows narrow-mindedness. It is the handwriting of a CEO and shows independence in the short *d* and *t* stems, as well as initiative in the breakaway *t* endings.

To cultivate open-mindedness, do this exercise over three days, keeping all the *e*'s wide open. If you happen to be at the beach, this exercise is fun to do in the sand (and if you do it with flair, it's likely to gain you a receptive audience).

Start by doing the open *e* relaxation exercise, without picking up the pen as you write across the page (see page 25).

Then proceed by drawing individual large lowercase *e*'s across the page. Exaggerate the loop part of the *e*. Make sure that it is free from any markings inside. Fill up the page (or the beachfront) with these very large *e*'s.

Individual lowercase e's drawn across the page help develop open-mindedness. Keep the loops plump.

On another page, draw *o*'s and *a*'s also without any markings inside the loops.

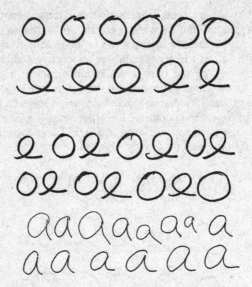

Adding *o*'s to the *e* formations reinforces open-mindedness.

Now write the following sentence on a page of white, unlined paper:

Only a receptive mind can be touched by exquisite poetry.

Next, fill up two pages of connected *e*'s, keeping the loops open and clean.

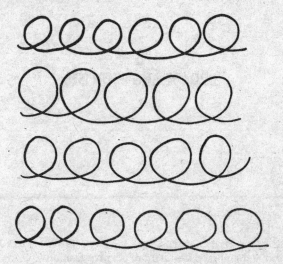

Connected *e's* for open-mindedness are similar to the *e*-form relaxation exercise. The difference is that here you try to keep the *e's* as "fat" as possible.

6
BROADENING EXERCISES

THIS SET OF FIVE EXERCISES WILL HELP YOU EXPAND INTO YOUR world and embrace it in a more positive fashion.

ENTHUSIASM

Enthusiasm is eagerness and ardor, most often with a sense of passion and excitement. Enthusiasm implies possibility and belief. If these qualities aren't present in the thinking process, enthusiasm can't blossom. Possibility and belief support faith in a result that's worth pursuing.

Another way to look at enthusiasm, then, is as intense willpower. Enthusiasm is inspirational, and a lack of it may cause a personality to become sluggish. In this regard, enthusiasm is trusting that a beneficial result will follow from action—an assurance of things hoped for and a conviction that they will happen as hoped for.

Dynamism is an important aspect of enthusiasm. In business, enthusiasm is a hallmark of those who are most successful. It is often a characteristic of charismatic leadership. The enthusiastic individual responds to situations by rising to the occasion with verve. The underlying thought (which may not be conscious) is, "How can I respond most effectively?" The enthusiastic individual looks at life with an attitude that sees obstacles as challenges rather than as problems, and life situations as opportunities and possibilities. The enthusiastic individual, for example, views these graphotherapy exercises as challenges that lead to prospects and potentials.

Enthusiasm is ultimately a fuel for action. It is indicated in handwriting by a long, sweeping *t* bar, which reflects the energy the writer feels beyond what is actually needed to accomplish the goal.

You'll hear in conversation that so and so has an enthusiasm for life, or so and so is an enthusiastic supporter of the arts, or so and so is an enthusiastic collector of sculpture, and so on. In most social situations, the enthusiastic person stands out, and others are interested because that passion is evident and compelling. The enthusiastic individual has the capabilities of inspiring others.

Look at the following handwriting samples. Notice how the stroke crosses the *t* bar in the illustrations. It is heavier than the others in the writing. This is typical of enthusiasm.

hat *cat*

mat *chat*

With Best

all that beauty all that wealth ere gave

Alike await the inevitable hour

the path of glory leads but to the grave

Thomas A Edison

These sweeping *t* bars show enthusiasm. Thomas Edison's is uncommonly enthusiastic and is one of my favorite samples.

The exercise for enthusiasm takes ten days. On the first day, make long, sweeping strokes of the *t* bar down a full page of unlined paper. Exaggerate the length and heaviness of each line.

On days two and three, write the whole *t*, exaggerating the sweeping nature of the *t* bar. Feel the energy coursing through your hand as you write. Press down as hard as you can on the *t* bar.

On days four, five, and six, write this sentence:

It takes time to truly attain.

Fill the page and sweep the *t* bars with great energy and verve. Make the *t* bars heavier than the rest of your writing.

If your name has a *t* in it, add your signature each time you write the sentence in this exercise. Of course, sweep the *t* bar in your signature and remember why you are doing this.

Many people actually smile and say they can't believe this will make them more enthusiastic. Then they look at their wimpy *t* bar, sweep the new one, and nod their heads positively.

On days seven through ten, fill up a page with *t*'s of many sizes. Be sure to keep sweeping the *t* bars. Throughout the exercise, don't expect suddenly to become a wildly passionate person. Enthusiasm has many levels. What will happen is that you will become more aware of your ability to embrace life, and this trait will help you to put yourself across to others in a more positive light. In your enthusiasm, you may realize that this exercise can't easily be shared with others!

On day one, write only *t* bars across a page.

On days two and three, write the entire *t* with an exaggerated movement.

If your name has a *t* in it, write it with a sweeping bar.

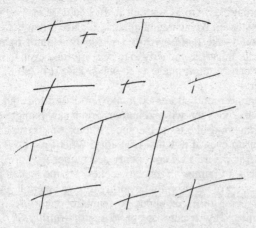

On days seven through ten, fill up a page with *t*'s of many sizes.

Try to make this an ongoing exercise.

A major food company sent me the handwriting of a potential sales manager. Lonny Franklin had all of the necessary requisites for the job, but at the interview he couldn't sell himself to the personnel manager. The company agreed to have Lonny come to my office for two sessions. He told me that he had recently gone through a divorce, and it affected every aspect of his life. I then explained the concept of behavior modification and how it could help him get the job he wanted. He worked very hard on this trait and then returned for another interview. The personnel manager was very impressed with his persistence and determination to get the job, and he was hired.

SENSE OF HUMOR

Humor is many things: fun, merriment, jocularity, levity, mirth, high spirits. The best of all, however, may be the ability to laugh, even at oneself, especially in tough situations. Humor is salvation, a steam valve, and even a tool for survival. Imagine a world without it. It would be at least dull and might well be austere and harsh, a place where individuals would take themselves too seriously. Humor lightens the world. It has the capacity to raise spirits and even to heal. Humor can certainly make even one's darkest hours a little brighter.

Sigmund Freud addressed humor in his writings but differentiated between wit and humor. Freud saw humor as an overriding God-like trait. To Freud, humor was the epitome of maturity even if a denial of reality. What Freud referred to as wit is the trait we commonly call humor.

A sense of humor offers many benefits to the human psyche. It can provide us with the ability to avoid mental ruts. It allows seeing other or opposing points of view in a non-threatening way. It permits one to see the futility of being defined or invalidated by others' thoughts and feelings.

Humor lets us try to get a grasp on what is not in our control and which may be frightening or frustrating. For example, death and sex are the basis of much humor because these are things largely out of human control. The sense of humor is also what protects self-esteem.

Having a healthy sense of humor is essential to personal happiness. Psychological tests have shown that the most self-actualized, happy people score high in appreciation of a sense of humor.

One can develop a sense of humor, which is essential medicine for a discouraging world.

Humor is represented in handwriting by an initial flourish on *m*'s and *n*'s that is not ostentatious. It usually blends softly into the next downstroke. Flourishes can be seen in any letter but are seen most often in capital *M*'s and *N*'s.

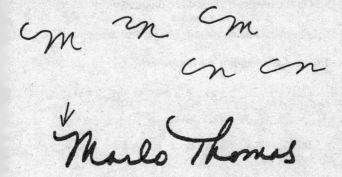

Humor strokes can take many forms but usually appear on *m*'s and *n*'s, as shown. Actress Marlo Thomas has a prominent humor flourish, as you can see in this sample below the strokes.

The exercise for developing humor takes four days. For the first two days, write a full page of capital and lowercase *m*'s and *n*'s with an initial flourish.

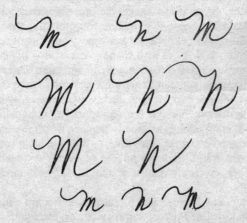

Fill a page with *m*'s and *n*'s that have the humor flourish.

On the next two days, write this sentence:

Noble men and mirthful maids make merry.

Fill a page, including all flourishes.

Noble men and mirthful maids make merry

This sentence, filling up an entire page, encourages humor.

IMAGINATION

There is a song, the opening of which states: "Imagination is funny, it makes a cloudy day sunny." This short phrase speaks volumes about the capacity and power of imagination.

Technically, imagination is the conscious mental process of evoking ideas or images of objects, events, relations, attributes, or processes never before experienced or perceived. It is the forming of images by combining the various elements of your experience in memory and an entirely creative aptitude that can give shape to everything in your personal universe. By directing your imagination toward what it is you want, you can transform every phase of your life.

Psychologists sometimes distinguish between two types of imagination: passive (or reproductive) imagination, in which mental images originally perceived by the senses are elicited, and active, constructive, or creative imagination, in which the mind produces images of events or objects that are either insecurely related or unrelated to past and present reality.

When an imagined and a real perception are simultaneous, the imagined perception may be confused with or even mistaken for the true perception. In any event, imagination is a part of cognition, which is the process of knowing.

Children are especially imaginative because their cognition is relatively unencumbered by facts and the other realities of life that we learn as we mature. Children haven't learned not to imagine; imagining is a normal state of being for them. The products of imagination so natural to children are fantasies, dreams, and fancies that are actualized in the fertile field of the mind. To some degree, imagination is brought forward into adulthood. For example, the pioneering psychologist and analyst Carl Jung developed an inclination for dreaming and fantasy during his lonely childhood that greatly influenced his adult work. Jung showed the parallels between ancient myths and disordered fantasies and explained human motivation in terms of a larger creative, imaginative energy.

Reconnecting with childhood imagination can be valuable in unlocking the imaginative potential you have as an adult. Try to remember the kind of things you imagined when you were a child. What games did you play that relied on imaginative elements?

Even if we, as adults, personally downplay our imagination, the evidence of its necessity and desirability in society is demonstrable everywhere. On a grander scale, imagination plays an important role in the relationship between our myths and knowledge. Myths may be studied from an intellectual and logical viewpoint, but ultimately it is the imaginative, intuitive side of myths that give the power of meaning to them. Also, culturally, without imagination there would be no entertainment industry. Films, games, music, theater, you name it, would not exist without imagination.

Creativity is a vital partner with imagination. It is a goal-directed search for solutions to a problem or challenge resulting in a discovery of some form of positive resolution. It is an activity of individuals (even if working in partnership) that involves cognitive, emotional, and motivational processes.

Imagination plays an important role in inventing something new and innovative. In the cognitive aspect of creativity, the mental states involved process information. It is the motivational and emotional aspects that initiate the creative process and move it to completion. From a scientific point of view, the ways that thoughts can be assembled in the human brain are immense. For example, in the hierarchical organization of speech alone, the number of possible sentences that may appear in ordinary conversation is vast. The implication of this is that not only is the human creative potential vast but also that your own creative potential is equally huge and can be developed and applied to benefit all aspects of your life.

Creative imagination requires the use of your will (see page 144). This faculty can be trained, and it will grow through exercise.

Picturing or visualizing a desire is wonderful as long as you are consistent. Always try to imagine success and positive scenarios. Don't allow negative images to come into your mind.

Creative imagination is found in handwriting in large lower loops.

g y j jury gong

giving it a try

Large lower loops as shown in the letters above indicate creativity and imagination. The samples of writing above belong to individuals with imagination.

and dependability. I have many acquaintances and few good friends. I am very selective (critical) in choosin

following along to the beat of some one else's drumming is ok for some, yet I think we each

The potential for creative imagination diminishes as the loop compresses. A line without a loop demonstrates a very practical attitude toward life. These individuals know best what they can feel and touch. They also tend to prefer to be alone.

Exaggerated lower loops, on the other hand, show that boundaries have been crossed into the realms of exaggeration and overstatement.

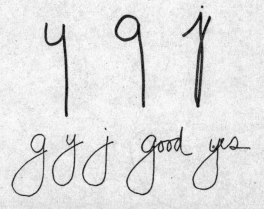

A compressed lower loop (top) indicates a diminishing potential for creative imagination. Exaggerated lower loops (bottom) indicate a tendency toward overstatement.

There is another kind of imagination related to the upper loops in handwriting, particularly the letters *b*, *h*, and *l*. This is the area of conceptual and abstract thinking as well as one's ability to perceive and embrace philosophical, metaphysical, and spiritually based ideas.

If the loops are inflated, there is an openness to embracing these concepts with imagination. The potential diminishes as the loop compresses. The taller the loops, the more likely the writer explores mysterious areas that may intimidate most people. Thus, great philosophers and religious leaders, as well as other original thinkers, typically demonstrate large upper loops. If there are inverted V formations on top of the upper loops, there is a tendency to be curious and questioning.

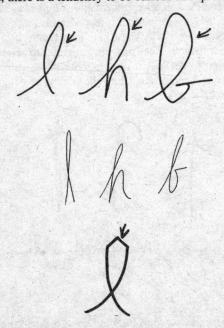

Philosophical and intellectual capacity is shown in full upper loops (top). An inverted V in an upper loop (bottom) shows curiosity.

The exercise to stimulate creative imagination takes five days to complete. On days one and two, fill up a page with long and wide lower loops on *g*'s, *y*'s, and *j*'s. Make sure the upstroke always goes back up through the baseline of writing. This brings up to reality the potential application of your imaginative ideas. Exaggerate the loops at first. Make them much fuller than you would ordinarily.

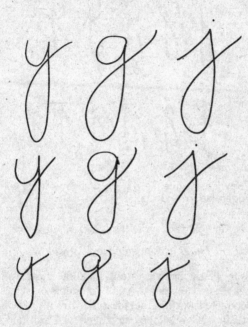

On the first two days, fill a page with *g*'s, *y*'s, and *j*'s with long, very wide lower loops.

On day three, fill up a page of these letters with full but not exaggerated loops.

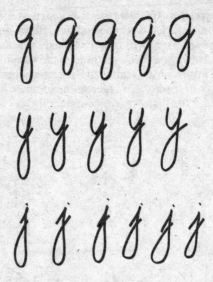

On day three, write the g's, y's and j's with full but not
exaggerated lower loops.

On days four and five, write the following sentence:

Imagine a juggler juggling yams.

Make sure that your loops are full and the upstroke returns
to the baseline. How did you feel doing this exercise?

Incomplete loops indicate ideas that haven't been brought
up to reality. If your loops stop short and are incomplete,
slowly progress to full loops that come up straight through
the baseline.

If you can locate the John Lennon song "Imagine," end
your exercise playing it.

OPTIMISM

Optimism embraces hope, brightness, happiness, enthusiasm, assurance, cheerfulness, expectation, and faith. Opti-

mists are often able to dismiss many of their fears of today by looking forward to goals that will work for them tomorrow.

The classic example of an optimist is the general who, in a heavy enemy attack, announced to his troops: "We're not retreating, we're advancing in another direction." Putting this spin on the event places it in a more positive, helpful light!

Some people claim to be neither optimists nor pessimists but realists, which supposes that optimists and pessimists are not committed to rationally estimating, but rather to underestimating or overestimating good outcomes. Yet both optimists and pessimists believe that they are realists; what is actually happening is that each position provides more than detached assessments of objective probability. Optimism and pessimism are specific modes of cognition and action—in other words, action-guiding attitudes. Each affects a person's thinking, behavior, happiness, and achievement.

Optimism can help you not only accept an event for what it is, or appears to be, but also change the focus so you can concentrate on what can be learned from the event, what opportunities it opens up, and what benefits can be drawn from it, instead of seeing it as an unpleasant, annoying, impossible obstacle. Optimism can also teach you how a recurrence can be prevented because you refuse to be focused on the negatives.

Optimists realize that growth requires some frustrations and setbacks and that learning what works is often impossible without taking paths that lead to dead ends. Therefore, optimists focus on the goal, regarding setbacks along the way as opportunities to progress and overcome fear(s). Such an approach fosters an attitude in which you are motivated and persistent in trying again until you succeed. Instead of getting hung up in problems, optimism allows you to spend your time constructively looking for ways to solve them.

Another way to characterize optimism is as a positive, as opposed to negative, approach. To choose the negative approach is to dwell on what is wrong, which has potentially detrimental consequences for you.

Optimists dislike obstacles to their plans. Consequently, they question limitations, accepting limits as limits in a context and then widening the context to step around the obstacle through the application of reason, analysis, and/or creative thinking.

Looking at the world with optimism is energizing—it encourages cheerfulness and activity. Optimism also feeds on itself in a positive way. The enthusiasm resulting from optimism tends to lead to effort and progress, which generate more optimism. Hence, optimism is forward-looking and self-improving. The activity is ongoing, a constant process of growth, self-correction, and improvement. Since optimists have positive expectations, they control fear, especially fear of failure, of being wrong, or of making mistakes. In this regard, optimism encourages experimentation. Optimism permits a search for better solutions, for finding ways to overcome barriers, and an openness to new sources of information with respect to improving life.

In handwriting, optimism is shown in an upward sloping of the letters, particularly the *t* bar.

Martin Luther King, Jr. and Jacqueline Onassis showed key signs of optimism in their writing. Trace or copy the writing of these individuals and experience how writing in their style makes you feel. Is it comfortable for you? Write your reactions in your notebook.

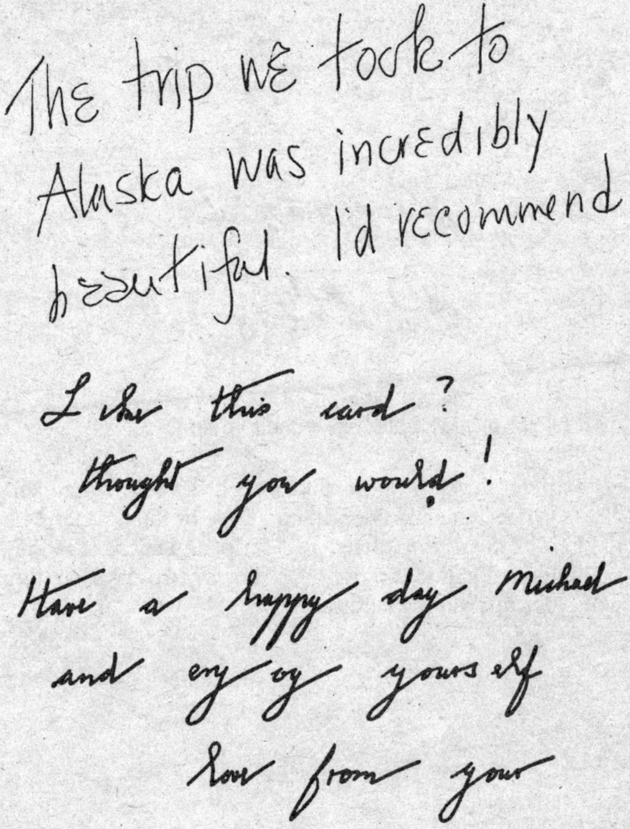

The trip we took to
Alaska was incredibly
beautiful. I'd recommend

I like this card?
thought you would!

Have a happy day Michael
and enjoy yourself

love from your

These samples show optimism in the handwriting, indicated by upward slopes.

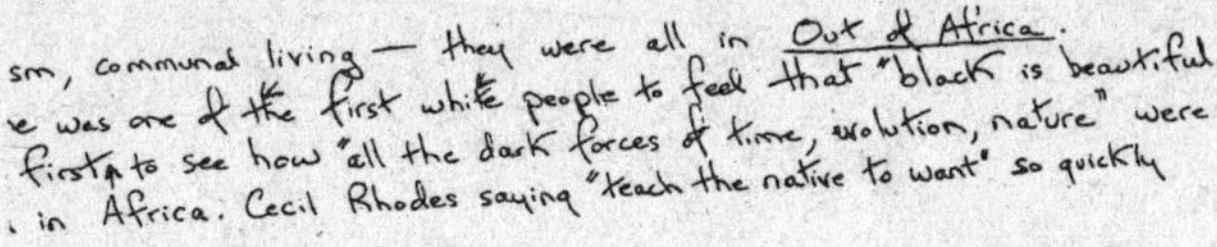

sm, communal living — they were all in _Out of Africa_.
ie was one of the first white people to feel that "black is beautiful."
first, to see how "all the dark forces of time, evolution, nature" were
, in Africa. Cecil Rhodes saying "teach the native to want" so quickly

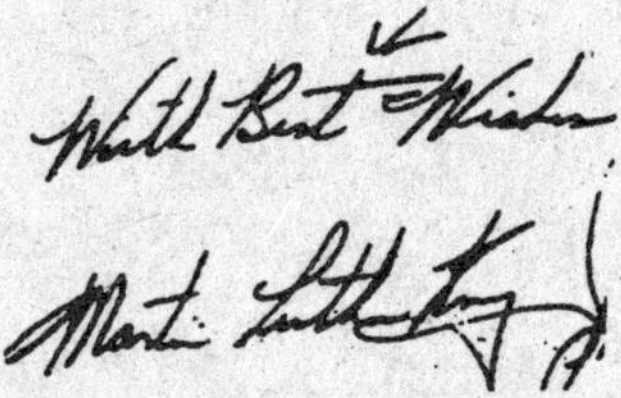

With Best Wishes

Martin Luther King, Jr.

Jacqueline Onassis (top) and Martin Luther King, Jr. (bottom) display optimism in their writing.

You can develop optimism through the following exercise. On days one and two, fill up a page of lined paper with *t*'s, half of them printed and half scripted, and be sure they point upward and to the right. Do this for two days, starting with your relaxation exercises.

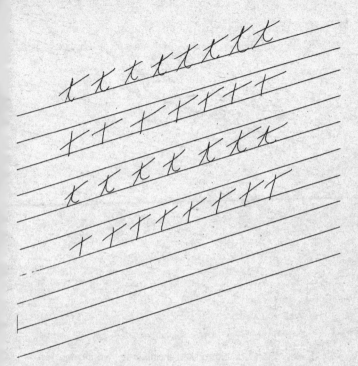

On days one and two, fill up a page with *t*'s with the *t* bar sloping upward.

Next, write the following sentence on lined paper, with the *t* bars sloping upward.

Optimism is hope for the best.

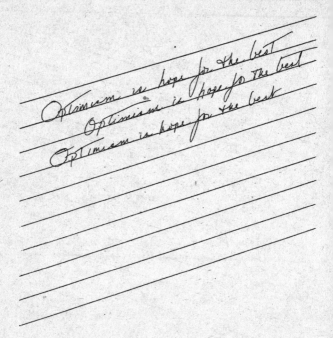

Follow the *t* bar exercise with this one, writing the sentence on lined paper.

On days three and four, write a page of the sentence on *unlined* paper. Make sure the words in the sentence are either level with the baseline or slope upward and to the right.

Optimism is hope for the best

On days three and four, write the sentence on unlined paper.

EXPANSION

Expansion is increase, enlargement, and growth. An expansive person is able to encompass the entirety of his or her environment. At the root of expansion is momentum, which permits movement toward growth. In physics, momentum is the fundamental quality characterizing the motion of any object. In accordance with Isaac Newton's laws of motion, if no external force acts on a body, its momentum is conserved—stopped. Likewise, without the force of the will to propel you, there is no momentum and no expansion. Momentum thus allows forward movement to build on itself. It is a continuum of energy that allows sustained action outward.

By contrast, short bursts of energy result in a single isolated action. Such single actions may address a particular issue, but they don't provide the impetus required for continuous growth and expansion where every action, whether successful or not, adds additional energy outward into an expansive pattern of growth. Therefore, you continually work toward creating eventual success.

Developing expansiveness allows you to see the bigger picture and fill up your world with meaningful experiences.

Expansiveness is found in the handwriting in a combination of traits. This means that in any one handwriting considered expansive, several traits are taken together to reach this conclusion. These traits may not necessarily be the same for all handwriting that is expansive. For example, one expansive handwriting may contain broad-mindedness (open *e*'s, *o*'s and *a*'s), enthusiasm (sweeping *t* bars), and imagination (full lower or upper loops). Another sample may contain investigative thinking patterns (wedged *m*'s, *n*'s and *h*'s) and imagination, coupled with a supratype slant (slightly to the right).

O have been working in

This sample shows expansiveness and investigative
thinking in this combination: supratype plus slant, clear
o's and a's; open e's, upward slant from the baseline,
full lower and upper loops.

It was always Kate Meehan's dream to own at least one
restaurant and, preferably, a chain of them. Kate is a
gourmet chef who wanted to develop entrepreneurial skills.
She was held back from her dream, although she couldn't
pinpoint this when she came to me, because of a limitation
in her vision. She had goals but didn't know how to put them
into effect. Her handwriting showed some confusion.

Kate had been brought up in a family without leadership.
Even though she had strong traits, she always positioned
herself as a follower. Graphotherapy allowed Kate to see
beyond her immediate environment. Her program of therapy
included working for months on opening up, decision-making (commitment), and determination. Today, Kate has
opened a restaurant and is planning her second.

*I will be leaving for ____
on the 30th and I'm feeling
pressured by my clients &, I guess,
life in general. I want to use
the 2½ weeks I'll be gone to clear
my head & consider what my
next career move should hence
my desire to see you before I go.*

Kate's handwriting is expansive (right slant, optimism,
clear o's and a's, full lower loops, analytic thinking) but
also contains some confusion in the way the words overlap each other from line to line.

The following short exercise will help you expand. Copy the drawing, filling up a minimum of two pages. Start with small loops and spiral them larger and larger across the page, keeping the pen on the page in a fluid motion. Ask yourself: What does it feel like to be expansive?

In addition, write your signature starting very small and expanding each time until it is very large. Fill up an entire page.

While you are doing both exercises, imagine yourself expanding into the entire room you occupy as you write.

Drawing spirals promotes qualities of expansion.

(*continued*)

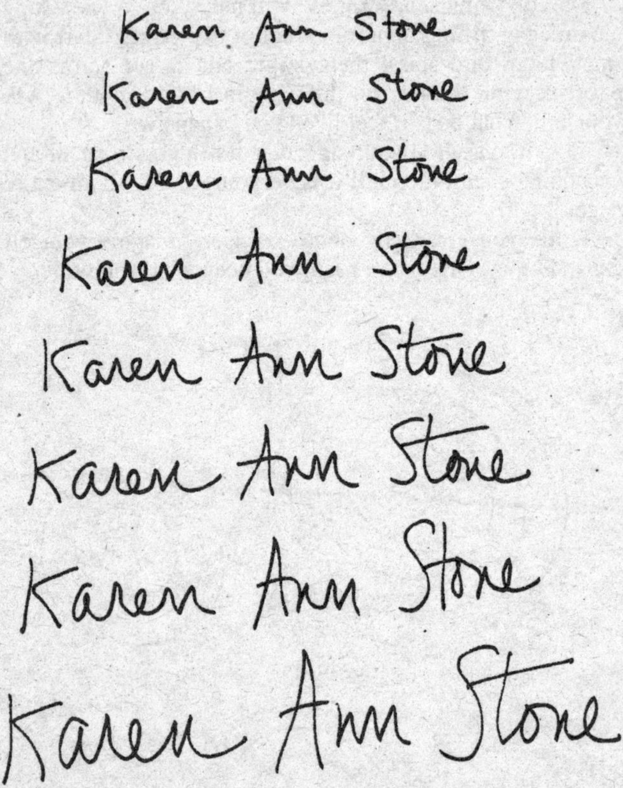

Karen Ann Stone
Karen Ann Stone
Karen Ann Stone
Karen Ann Stone
Karen Ann Stone
Karen Ann Stone
Karen Ann Stone
Karen Ann Stone

Writing your name larger and larger down a page also
helps you to expand.

7
INTENSIFYING EXERCISES

THIS SERIES OF SIX EXERCISES IS DESIGNED TO STRENGTHEN and intensify positive action traits. They'll help you navigate your world with gumption and dynamism.

PERSISTENCE

Persistence is the dogged pursuit of a goal or a course of action, sometimes in the face of opposition or lack of interest. It is perseverance and stick-to-itiveness, the kind that gets the job done no matter what. Things that persist or endure are said to be lasting. Thus, persistence implies momentum that is ongoing. A measure of persistence is how often we try and try again until we complete our intention.

One element of persistence is endurance. In physical fitness, endurance is the ability of the body to meet demands imposed by the environment. The same definition can be applied to persistence: It is the ability of the mind or intellect to meet the demands imposed in a cognitive environment. The parallels between physical endurance and mental endurance are noteworthy. Both involve pushing the limits of the body or mind and staying with the task until it's finished. Marathon runners, for instance, have great endurance.

Likewise, they have persistence—without either they wouldn't be able to conclude this race of more than twenty-six miles.

Individuals with persistence are driven by a need for completion. They desire closure; they won't give up. But what separates individuals who are so motivated from those who are not? There are many possibilities, resulting from societal, environmental and behavioral sources. Here are some examples of how and why individuals develop persistence:

- experience harsh environments where survival depends on not giving up
- encouraged by parents/authority figures to achieve and excel
- are natural risk-takers—enjoy challenges
- low self-esteem—a way to prove worth
- high self-esteem—self-satisfaction in seeing a job done well
- perfectionism

No matter what the motivating force, persistence is a trait worth cultivating for those who tend to quit too soon. President Calvin Coolidge once said:

Nothing in the world can take the place of persistence.
Talent will not; nothing is more common than unsuccessful men with talent.
Genius will not; unrewarded genius is almost a proverb.
Education will not; the world is full of educated derelicts.
Persistence and determination alone are omnipotent.

In handwriting, persistence is indicated by tie strokes. A tie stroke goes to the left, then ties through the letter on its way to the right. These strokes are usually located in *f*'s and *t*'s, but they show up in other letters as well.

$$\cancel{f} \quad \cancel{+} \quad A \quad H$$

Benjamin Disraeli was once asked to define the difference between a tragedy and a catastrophe. After a moment's

I had fun in the City, but it is time to visit the Country.

Frankly, I fear if I go forward

Tie strokes show persistence. They are most common in *f*'s and *t*'s but can show up in other letters as well. These samples all show persistence, seen in the various tie strokes.

The exercise for persistence is done over five days. On day one, write a line of *f*'s with tie strokes. On the next line write *t*'s with tie strokes. Alternate the *f*'s and *t*'s for a full page. Write larger than usual.

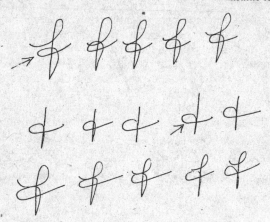

Practicing tie strokes will help develop persistence.

On days two and three, copy this sentence exactly in your natural-size script, including all the tie strokes.

If at first you fail, try until you sail.

If you find this exercise difficult, write another page of tie strokes. Keep developing your stick-to-itiveness until you are able to see this exercise through.

INITIATIVE

Initiative is taking the first step or the lead, without being urged. It's the act of setting a process or chain of events in motion. Self-starters have initiative and the ability to be independent and enterprising. Leaders of successful enterprises almost always take the initiative in order to succeed—they are proactive rather than reactive. This approach allows them to make choices that lead to productive change instead of just waiting for things to happen.

This notion of taking charge, whether it is taking responsibility for one's own actions, career, health, or life, is essential to personal growth. However, it's important to realize that true initiative begins with taking charge of yourself—

your mind, your emotions, your thoughts, and your body. All other events emanate outward from this. If you are not truly in some level of control of yourself, your ability to be an initiator can be seriously compromised. For example, if you are in business, how can you expect to gain promotion if you procrastinate, are chronically late, or engage in any activity that demonstrates your lack of self-control?

The famous sneaker ad enjoins us to "just do it." If we have initiative we can indeed go out and do it. Many people know what they want, and they know what it takes to fulfill these needs. Most people probably have the resources to attain what they've defined for themselves as desirable. Yet many never do it. Many gifted people have never developed initiative, and their dreams wait forever for others to build them.

Initiative implies the willingness to forgo the comfort of the known and take risks. This is a choice made in the moment of decision. Instead of playing it safe, the person with initiative opts to take control, take charge, and act.

Initiative is shown in handwriting by stroke forms known as "breakaways." These strokes are written upward and to the right. The closer the stroke is to being straight, and the more forcefully it departs from the preceding stroke, the more powerful the initiative. Look for breakaway strokes throughout the writing. However, they are most often observed in an uncrossed *t* that is usually in the last letter in a word.

Initiative is shown by breakaway strokes.

The exercise to strengthen initiative should be done for at least five consecutive days.

First, fill up two pages with lowercase *t*'s, including straight breakaways. Feel the energy coursing through as you sharply break away the stroke.

Next, write a page of the following sentence:

What great feat might we expect?

Make sure all the *t*'s have straight breakaway strokes.

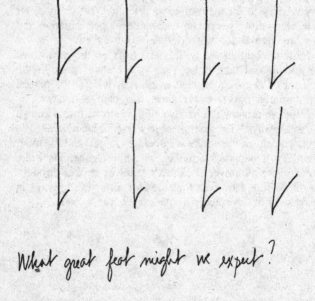

What great feat might we expect?

Practice breakaway strokes with vigor to develop initiative.

This exercise looks deceptively easy. However, initiative is a forceful action that requires strength, determination, and courage behind it.

As a supplementary exercise for initiative, set a goal yourself to do something that you are encouraged to do but haven't yet accomplished. Take the initiative and see how you feel as you work to achieve your goal. Write down all feelings at the end of the exercise and refer to these notes the next day. Think of the breakaway stroke and position the word *initiative* in your mind.

DETERMINATION

Determination is firmness of mind, resolve, and conviction. It's the quality that gives you the drive to move forward by taking definitive action, sometimes with mental toughness.

Determination implies the ability to take control of a situation, which in turn means that you have to be willing to take responsibility for your actions and the fulfillment of your objective(s). Thus, you achieve because you realize you must act on a situation yourself—no one is going to do it for you.

Another aspect of determination is the desire to overcome limits. A determined person might ask what is possible and what is not. Such a person might question traditional limitations in pursuit of a goal because his or her personality is geared to believe that any goal is possible. This is the spirit of determination.

Yet another important element of determination is commitment. Without commitment, there is hesitancy, holding back. With commitment comes a decision and the potential for an entire stream of events to emanate from it. Commitment drives the action necessary for a determination to be carried out. The degree of your commitment indicates the depth of your determination and your ability to follow through, to see a course of action through to a conclusion, and sometimes beyond. This extends the arc of the action farther into the future, with the potential for greater result. In other words, if you take an action and envision the full completion of the motion, you are likely to arrive at your goal straighter and sooner.

Determination is an action-driven, dynamic state of mind, shown in handwriting by very firm, straight downstrokes in the letters *g*, *y*, and *j*. The downstrokes must be written without a curve, and they may or may not have loops. If your downstrokes are curved, don't expect an immediate result from this exercise. Work at it diligently, however, until your downstrokes are gradually straightened.

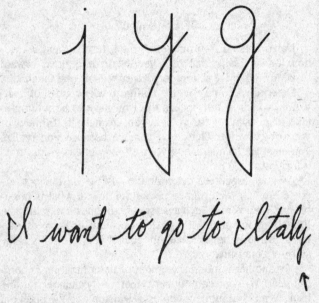

Determination is shown by firm and straight downstrokes.

The exercise for determination takes five days. On the first day, write a page of downstrokes about twice their normal length, keeping them as straight as possible.

Write these downstrokes firmly at twice their normal length.

On day two, write the downstrokes in your normal handwriting size.

Now write the strokes at their normal size, keeping them straight and firm.

On days three to five, write this sentence, making sure the downstrokes are straight:

Steady goes it till my job is done.

This sentence helps develop determination.

You will know you have mastered the trait of determination when you have firm, blunt downstrokes on your *y*'s, *g*'s, and *j*'s.

DECISIVENESS

Decisiveness is that part of decision-making which allows you to make a commitment to a thought, concept, action, philosophy, plan, relationship, etc. Decision-making, from the simplest to the most complex levels, is comprised of the following activities:

1. identification of the criteria involved in the decision
2. prioritization of these criteria
3. evaluation of the criteria

The evaluation phase of the process encompasses a number of subprocesses, including data, what-if and risk analysis; examination of options and critical factors; and the creation of assumptions and possible outcomes. The result of these activities is a decision. The decisive individual:

- assumes responsibility for most major areas of his or her life
- expresses disagreement without fear of loss of support or approval
- initiates projects
- undertakes activities on his or her own
- has self-confidence in judgments made

Decisive individuals are definitive and conclusive. Their decision-making is marked by a clear, positive, and confident manner. When goals are identified, there is the ability to achieve them in an assured manner, without hesitation.

Decisive actions move forward to conclusions, though nobody can guarantee that decisiveness necessarily brings on the *right* conclusions. If you prefer conclusions to endless vacillations, postponed choices among myriad options, and stagy gestures, then this is the exercise for you. Being able to conclude thoughts and intentions with decisiveness saves time.

Years ago I attended a sales seminar at Marymount College in New York City. One point made that day that I have never forgotten was: *Maybe* is a word that connotes useless indecision. Accept no maybes, just yes or no. Anyone who sells is statistically better off getting a straight yes or no decision immediately. A yes can be celebrated, a no can be changed or accepted, but a maybe postpones action and is accepted mostly by those who fear hearing a no and who take a no as final.

The trait of decisiveness is indicated in handwriting by sturdy, firm endings to words, which may increase in weight or even form a knob where the stroke ends.

We are pretty well settled into a regular schedule. I decided not to monkey around waiting for the school to decide on a morning Mass schedule for the kids. So,

Make a joyful noise unto the Lord, all ye lands. Serve the Lord with gladness: come before his presence with singing. Know ye that the Lord he is God:

These two samples show decisiveness in their strong endings.

(*continued*)

sweet little Sheila, you know her if you see her,

y often Because it Hurts and I children, all my children all over

Best wishes

Bill Clinton

9-21-92

The three samples on this page have weak, indecisive endings. The last is President Bill Clinton's writing; he has often been criticized for being indecisive.

If the endings on your letters are already firm and fully extended, then this exercise can be skipped. If your letter endings are less firm than you wish, this exercise can be of help and act as a reinforcement. Start the decisiveness exercise by doing several relaxation exercises of your choosing and one page of the concentration exercise. Then do one page of the asterisk drawing on unlined paper.

Complete each line on the asterisk with an abrupt ending. Do this exercise very slowly and pay close attention to balance. This exercise will also help you to maintain your self-discipline.

Each time you make a line in the asterisk, finish it with a very abrupt ending.

Next, fill a page, starting with very large asterisks. As you go down the page, make them smaller and smaller, always with the endings firm. The smaller ones are more challenging and may try your patience. If this starts to happen, find your exercise for humor and do a page or two.

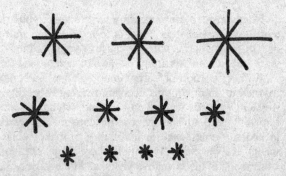

After practicing the asterisk drawing, fill a page with asterisks that start large and end small.

Finally, do one page of single words all with the blunt endings. On the second page, incorporate the words into sentences relating to the topic. Do this for two days.

could   when   hat   can

that   yes   part   hair   cā

When can you buy a hat?

yes I can buy that hat

Part that hair in the

Write a page of words with blunt endings. Then incorporate them into sentences.

Now consider situations in your life when you are hesitant to make decisions. What accounts for your indecisiveness? Come to terms with the cause of your hesitancy. Write your thoughts on this after you have completed the exercise.

A major portion of Larry Kempton's graphotherapy was devoted to improving his decision-making capability. Larry frequently couldn't make up his mind, which was a serious impediment to advancement in his career. Larry essentially lacked self-confidence in his ability to make sound judgments. He was severely criticized by his parents for decisions made in his formative years, and this carried over into his adulthood. He subconsciously saw his parents in all authority figures and, as a result, feared that decisions he made would be similarly discredited by senior management at his firm. Because he was not decisive, he was essentially paralyzed. My task was to build up Larry's confidence and improve his decision-making capability.

I have an interview tomorrow

Larry's handwriting shows an inability to make decisions. The left slant further inhibits him from putting himself forward in the world.

Indecisive individuals are held back. They are not able to make decisional commitments. They lack the abilities identified above. The reasons for this may be varied, such as a personality or learning dysfunction, but most are generally fear-based, as were Larry's. Fears are emotions that keep us from advancing. They are learned responses that trigger apprehension, anxiety, alarm, panic, and other nonproductive behaviors that block forward movement. The objective of the decisiveness exercises is to stimulate your ability to make decisions. It will help you make the commitments that allow you to move ahead.

To make the exercise for decisiveness most effective, do the complete set in the morning *and* in the evening, starting off with relaxation exercises of your choice. As always, remember to fill out your log.

DIRECTNESS

Directness is the ability to come straight to the point in thinking and acting. It is a lack of extraneous action. The ability to be direct implies direction, which permits you to live your life purposefully. As we live day to day we engage in a process of self-generated action in which we constantly make choices. Directness and purpose help you effectively enact those choices.

Directness is also related to assertiveness, which is the

ability to stand up for your own basic rights without violating the rights of others. Assertiveness is one of three recognized response styles. The other two are passivity, in which an individual may be submissive or resigned and thus unable to be direct, and aggression, in which the individual is overly direct in a hostile or combative way.

Developing directness helps you tackle an issue, deal with it, and move on to the next issue without wasting time. There is no mental hesitancy or stuttering. With directness, approach to work as well as relationships should be uncomplicated. Verbal communication is forthright.

In business, directness can be an asset—although it must, at times, be tempered by tact and diplomacy. Being overly direct enters into the blunt range, which may get offensive.

Directness is shown in handwriting in simple letter formations made without an approach (or lead-in) stroke or decorations.

I have enclosed handwriting of

What to look for in an accounting firm:
Are the people involved setting to understand
your business.

These samples, with no approach strokes, show directness.

To start the exercise, for five days write the entire alphabet (only lowercase letters) without any approach strokes.

a b c d e f g h i j k l m n o

p q r s t u v w x y z

Write the entire alphabet like this to develop directness.

Next, do two pages of the following drawing, being consistent as to size, shape, and spacing. This coherence in retaining the form encourages directness by discouraging extraneous strokes in your writing.

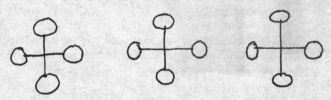

Try to be consistent when executing this drawing.

In addition, write a page of this sentence, also keeping your writing size and spacing the same:

I come to the point.

When you write the sentence, use no lead-in strokes (watch all of your writing for such strokes and eliminate them).

I Come to the point

This sentence helps develop directness.

Finally, do half a page of this drawing, which helps balance the left and right brain. Keep the points straight.

Try to keep the points straight as you execute this drawing for directness.

Keep up the directness exercises until you see the elimination of most of your initial strokes. In time you will find you can accomplish this with ease.

WILL

The French philosopher René Descartes uttered the famous statement, "I think, therefore I am," but it was the German philosopher Arthur Schopenhauer who extended the concept and said, "I will, therefore I am."

Will, in both philosophy and psychology, is the capacity to choose among alternative courses of action and act on the choice made, particularly when the action is directed toward a specific goal or is governed by definite ideals and principles of conduct. Willed behavior is different from behavior stemming from instinct, impulse, reflex, or habit, because none of these involves conscious choice. Psychologists tend to accept a pragmatic theory that the will is an aspect or quality of behavior (rather than a separate faculty). Individuals with sound effective wills are able to:

1. fix their attention on goals
2. adhere to sound principles of conduct

3. weigh alternatives and take deliberate action deemed the best way to achieve objectives
4. inhibit impulses and habits that might distract attention from, or otherwise conflict with, their aims
5. persevere against obstacles and frustrations

It is not fully known if strength of will is a matter of genetics. Some people appear to be born with greater powers of will—of attention and control—than others. However, environmental influences are of decisive importance in developing a strong will. The influence of home, school, and other institutional affiliations, plus an upbringing that stresses the importance of certain goals, ideals, and principles, tend to produce strong wills. Accommodation and being well-liked are much less likely to help an individual develop strength of will.

People who possess a strong will have a motivation toward accomplishment. They possess the volition to use the act of will to get things done. The willingness to do something is crucial to getting it done, and volition carries with it one's tremendous store of personal power. Willpower and self-starting ability are major leadership traits.

Willpower is shown in handwriting by relatively thick and weighty *t* bars that are usually placed between the middle and the top of the *t* stem. The thicker the *t* bar, the stronger the will.

The last two years I ha
used red, white, purple and
magenta petunias, mixing th
colors in rows or clusters a

The weighty *t* bar in this sample is a perfect illustration of the will trait.

Carol MacKenzie knew she had no willpower when it came to food. She didn't know when it would have occurred to her to stop eating of her own volition. Carol loved food and gratified her desire until she'd put 150 pounds on a short, small-boned frame. Her writing showed overall heavy pressure that indicted stress. Her *t* bars were relatively lightweight compared to the rest of her writing. They were low on the *t* stem, which indicates low estimation of self.

After evaluating her writing, Carol was given the exercises for will, concentration, and self-esteem. After several weeks of graphotherapy, Carol was able to admit that she was afraid to fail and scared of where success might take her. Carol is still working on exercises to help her control her fears and the desire to eat that stems from them. Fears may never truly leave, but one learns how to cope with them. Carol knows she has work to do, but she has, after six months, lost fifteen pounds.

we are a Systems Integrator since then. I starte working with them about 2.5 years ago. It wa very hard at the begining but now I love my job. Everymorning I just can not wait to get u and come to work. I work about 13/17 hour

The short, light *t* bars in Carol's handwriting show an undeveloped will.

The exercise to strengthen will takes seven days. First, write a page of *t*'s on unlined paper. Cross all of the *t* bars evenly on both sides of the stem and press down with medium to heavy pressure. Increase the weight of the bar as you advance down the page. Repeat on lined paper.

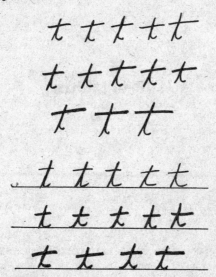

Write these *t* bars first on unlined paper, and then on lined paper.

Finally, write a page of this sentence on both lined and unlined paper:

I direct my will through my own control.

When writing this sentence, keep the *t* bars even and bold.

8
MASTERING EXERCISES

EVERYONE HAS PERSONALITY TRAITS THAT HE OR SHE WOULD like to eliminate or minimize. The following exercises address six traits that I commonly see in my practice, all of which can hold you back.

INHIBITION

Inhibition is a restraint, subjugation, or suppression of emotions and feelings, which, because they are bottled up, prevent you from expressing yourself fully and satisfactorily. Inhibitions can range in scope and depth from relatively minor, such as a woman feeling uncomfortable in a low-cut dress, to relatively serious, characterized by feelings such as inadequacy, extreme sensitivity to other people's attitudes, and social inhibition. Individuals who are severely inhibited may go so far as to avoid interpersonal contact, or become involved only where there is a certainty of being liked.

No matter what the extent of the inhibition, inhibited people tend to become overly self-absorbed and as a result stop themselves from taking risks or engaging in activities because they may prove embarrassing. In so doing, opportunities and potentials are cut off and are never experienced.

Life is thus diminished, and along with it the possibility of the joy, success, and fulfillment that are available to each and every one of us who will but reach for it.

Inhibition is mainly indicated in a leftward slant. Many people in the public eye have this trait, but they have learned to put themselves out nonetheless.

MEMORANDUM		Sept. 22nd 1976.
From	*To*	Mr. Craxton.
H.R.H. The Prince of Wales		

Please forgive the memo, but it is easier. Thank you for your letter outlining all your proposals for next year's exposure to the BBC. - what a daunting prospect for the poor, unsuspecting viewing public.

However, to take your points in order: -

1. I agree that rough guide lines are best at this stage. I have some basic ideas as to what I want to say and it may take a little longer than 5 minutes. It would help to have a look at any film you have before I write the final piece

2. a) Illustration section. A good idea to try and show a "before and after" situation with the Windsor gravel pit.

b). I am not altogether certain about this Australian or New Zealand illustration

(continued)

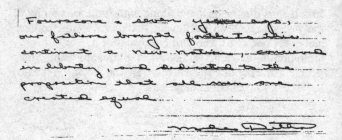

Fourscore a seven years ago, our fathers brought forth to this continent a new nation, conceived in liberty, and dedicated to the proposition that all men are created equal...

Matt Dillon

She was one of the first white people to feel that "black is beautiful." She was the first to see how "all the dark forces of time, evolution, nature" were being disrupted in Africa. Cecil Rhodes saying "teach the native to want" so quickly became Galbraith's "Affluent Society."

One of my favorite passages in _Out of Africa_ is where Isak Dinesen asks: "If I know a song of Africa, of the giraffe and the African new moon lying on her back of the plough in the fields and the sweaty faces of the coffee pickers, does

Inhibition is indicated by a left slant. Many public figures have this trait but have learned to overcome it. Prince Charles of England (page 149), Matt Dillon (top), and Jacqueline Kennedy Onassis (this page) all have a left slant.

Jackie Farber was not only inhibited, but she also had poor self-esteem, which led to issues surrounding any type of social interaction. She found it difficult to see other than the negative in life and had difficulty looking at situations objectively.

I met Jackie when something went terribly wrong in her life with which she couldn't adequately cope. Jackie was abandoned at the altar and discovered that her fiancé had eloped with another woman a week after she and he were to be married. This trauma reinforced Jackie's negative view of life and would have driven her further into herself had a caring friend (a former client of mine) not intervened.

In working with Jackie it was important to establish a rapport, make it clear that we were looking for a solution to her problem, and set limits for the counseling sessions. Otherwise, she might well have terminated our sessions before we could accomplish anything. Jackie's case was difficult but with slow and caring development, trust was built and Jackie began the process of coming out more into the world.

Jackie's writing initially showed poor self-esteem and inhibition (top). With much dedicated work, Jackie improved her outlook on life, reflected in the bottom sample. She also improved her outlook, raising her self-esteem and overcoming much of her inhibition.

The exercise for inhibition takes patience and care. Changing slant is very difficult and not recommended without the ongoing counseling of a certified graphotherapist. This is because the slant represents your fundamental, emotional core.

You can work on freeing your emotions by doing the following exercise. Fill up a page with this sentence:

I seek to expand into the world.

Write larger than you normally do and make sure you sweep the *t* bars (see the exercise for enthusiasm on page 104).

At the same time look at your capital *I*. If it slants to the left, work hard on writing it vertically. The left is the past, and what you are trying to accomplish is to bring yourself into the present and the future. You may also adjust the slant of your writing slightly to the right by writing every letter of the alphabet slanted vertically on lined paper. This may not feel natural and comfortable for you and may take a while to accomplish.

I seek to expand into the world

I seek to expand into the world

*a b c d e f g h i j k l
m n o p q r s t u v w x y z*

Writing with a vertical slant or a slant slightly veering to the right may feel uncomfortable if your slant is normally to the left, but the exercise will help you overcome inhibitions.

In conjunction with the exercise, plan a task daily that requires you to become involved with someone else. The task can be as complicated or as simple as you want. For example, you may plan a phone call and hold a conversation for a minimum set time. You may volunteer to do something worthy. You may join an acting class. The idea is to get out of yourself and interact with others.

STUBBORNNESS

Stubbornness is a trait that's fear based. It is a defense against loss of face. Many stubborn people are aware that their opinion is faulty but refuse to admit it and resist any effort to change their mind.

Stubbornness also implies rebelliousness, but without a just cause. It is rebelliousness for the sake of it and hence a perverse expression of individualism. Stubbornness is a disruptive force. The inflexibility involved in being stubborn can disrupt relationships of all kinds.

Stubbornness can be turned into determination and open-mindedness. The force of will that drives both can be negative (stubborn) or positive (determined).

In handwriting, stubbornness appears as a tent formation, in *d*'s and *t*'s mainly but also in *A* and *I* formations. The wider the wedge of the tent, the stronger the trait is within the personality of the writer.

The tent formation in a letter shows stubbornness.

Governor Mario Cuomo's handwriting shows some stubbornness. During his long and distinguished political career, he exercised this quality from time to time.

The exercise to overcome stubbornness takes six days to complete. *Several sets* of relaxation exercises are important to start this exercise. You should also do the exercise for open-mindedness in conjunction with this one. Open-mindedness is a great aid for relieving stubbornness.

For three days, on lined paper, fill up a half page with *d* and *t* letters only; keep the stems straight, without tent formations. Do not retrace the *t* stems.

On the second half of the page, write this sentence:

I strive to eliminate all signs of stubborn behavior.

d d d d d d d d

t t t t t t t t

I strive to eliminate all signs of stubborn behavior

Eliminating tent formations from your writing helps minimize stubbornness. Keep the *d*'s and *t*'s straight.

For the next three days, repeat the exercise on unlined paper, filling up the page. Repeat the persistence exercise as well as the one for open-mindedness along with this exercise.

PROCRASTINATION

Procrastination is the act of needlessly delaying tasks. Sometimes this occurs to such an extent that a great deal of discomfort or anxiety is produced. Procrastination means that your purpose seldom gets beyond the wishful thinking or good intentions stage. One may have a definite goal but may hesitate to start. People give many reasons for procrastinating, including:

- dislike or aversion to the task at hand
- frustration with performing the task
- not enough time to accomplish the task
- other tasks have more priority
- lack of interest
- too much to do
- too many distractions

These reasons are mostly superficial. Procrastination is known in graphology as a fear trait—that is, there is a deeper reason to procrastinate, born of some fear, such as a need to protect self-esteem or the fear of commitment.

Procrastination is almost always counterproductive, which is why it causes anxiety, which tends to feed on itself—the longer things don't get done, the more guilt the procrastination produces and, hence, the more anxiety.

With procrastination, aptitudes remain undeveloped, opportunities are lost, and talents can languish. Time management courses and other methods of overcoming procrastination frequently fail because they don't get at the root of the issue.

Procrastination is shown in handwriting by an incomplete *t* bar, disconnected from the *t* stem on its left side.

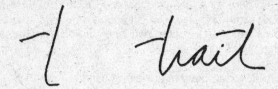

When the mail is sent to your address on the package it takes time to arrive in

The disconnected *t* bar at the left of the *t* stem shows procrastination. This handwriting sample shows an extreme amount of procrastination.

The exercise for procrastination takes ten days. Essentially, we replace procrastination with its antidote, following through—the ability to complete a task without pulling up short.

To help you begin the exercise and not procrastinate, it's helpful first to do the exercises for concentration, determination, and will. Also, do several relaxation exercises, as well as visualizations in which you see yourself committed to and completing tasks.

Start the exercise by writing a page of *t* bars to the left of the stem in the morning and completing the follow-through in the evening—that is, write the bars completely through the *t* stem. Do this for three days.

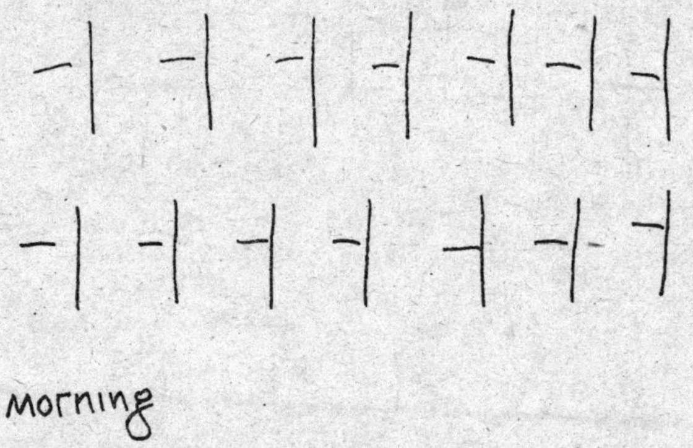

-| -| -| -| -| -|-| -|

-| -| -| -| -| -| -| -|

morning

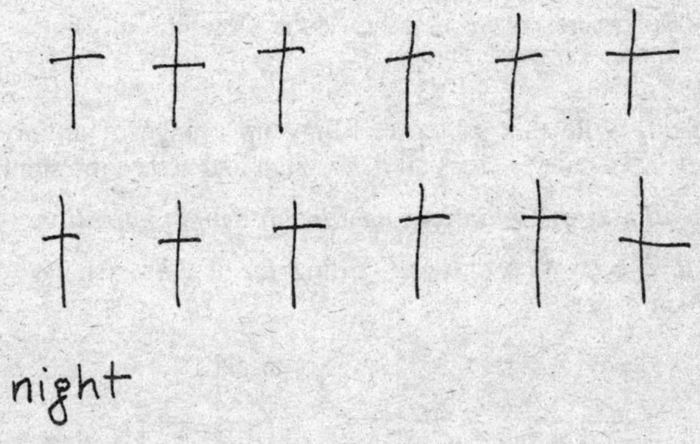

+ + + + + +

+ + + + + +

night

For the first three days, write a page of *t*'s with the bars
to the left of the stem in the morning. Follow through in
the evening by writing a page of *t*'s crossed all the way
through.

Then, for the remaining seven days, fill up two pages
with *t*'s crossed all the way through.

$$\dagger \dagger \dagger \dagger \dagger \dagger$$

$$t \ t \ t \ t \ t$$

Making sure the *t* is crossed all the way through helps eliminate procrastination.

Next, write this sentence, filling up a page of unlined paper. Take care to cross all *t*'s through and across the stem:

I will take the initiative and eliminate procrastination.

Now, copy this drawing, filling up at least a page of unlined paper.

At least a page of this drawing helps eliminate pro-crastination by building follow-through.

Finally, give yourself a small task to do every day. Try to complete the task, but if you fail, simply continue with the exercise until it becomes easier to follow through and accomplish your goal. If at the end of ten days you feel that you still need to work on follow-through, continue with the exercise until you achieve positive results.

CONFUSION

Confusion is an inability to be clear in thought and deed, which is the result of taking on too many tasks or commitments and/or having too much input/information to deal with at one time.

Confusion produces conflict in decision-making because of the pressure and stress of overload. Often there is a conflict between values, with the unsettling dilemma that a choice means sacrificing ideals or other objectives. To deal with such a predicament, individuals often avoid the decision altogether. Individuals with confusion in their handwriting benefit by incorporating some structure in their lives. It isn't that they can't deal with many things simultaneously, but that they need to focus on completing one at a time.

Confusion results in a lack of productivity. It also has a negative impact on your ability to be organized and to attend to details.

Confusion is shown in handwriting by lines of writing intruding on each other and getting tangled up, usually seen in upper and lower loops.

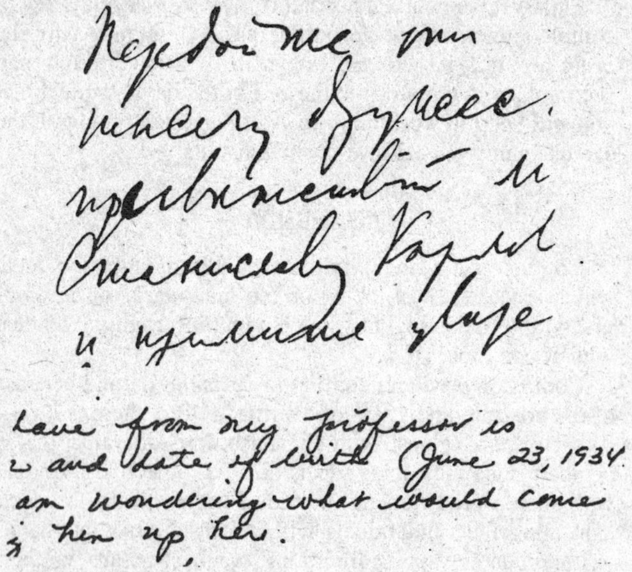

[handwritten text in Russian/Cyrillic script, illegible]

[handwritten text in English:] have from my professor is and date of birth (June 23, 1934 am wondering what would come him up, her.

The loops in both samples overlap words on the lines below, indicating confusion.

Ken McWilliams came to my office with one purpose in mind—to find the strength to stick to his twelve-step program. Ken was a compulsive gambler who'd been abstinent for about six months, was determined to stay in recovery, and already possessed plenty of energy and determination. His main problem was the amount of confusion and conflict in his handwriting, a result of the pressures of undertaking the recovery program and handling the other aspects of his life. To help siphon off the extra energy, Ken got involved in a physical exercise program along with our graphotherapy program. I started him out with a series of relaxation exercises and then proceeded to concentration and self-discipline. To help him deal with his confusion, and channel his determination in a positive direction, Ken concentrated on the exercise below. It helped him set priorities and goals as well as feel good about himself.

One of my chief concerns was to establish performance measures for our operations so that we could measure our performance over time and compare the company performance to that of our peers. We have adopted as many measures as possible that are utilized by the Steel Service Center Institute's Performance Analysis Report (PAR). Even so, the PAR is evolving. Information and analysis was financial; and now there is more customer focus to the information being gathered and analyzed in the PAR. Metal Treating Institute also has a similar report to the

Ken's handwriting showed confusion and conflict, mirroring the pressure he felt sticking to his twelve-step program.

The aim of this exercise is to eliminate confusion by providing the structure and routine that will help you identify what you want to accomplish and to complete tasks with clarity.

Begin this exercise by writing this sentence on lined paper:

I willingly deal with one thing at a time.

Keep the words well-spaced. Don't allow any of the letters to touch words above or below them. Be patient and take your time.

Do this exercise for three days. Then switch to unlined paper and do the exercise for another three days.

I willingly deal with one thing at a time.

I willingly deal with one thing at a time.

I willingly deal with one thing at a time.

I willingly deal with one thing at a time.

I willingly deal with one thing at a time.

Take your time when writing this sentence. Don't let an overlap occur.

In addition, make a list of tasks you must accomplish each day. Prioritize them by level of importance. Check off the tasks as you complete them. Do not do more than one task at a time.

REPRESSION

In a state of repression, we subconsciously push down unwanted thoughts, feelings, and experiences. Repression is a natural coping mechanism that can either serve or hinder depending on the nature of what is being repressed and the underlying reasons for doing so.

In its fundamental state, repression is usually an unconscious function that maintains equilibrium in the individual by sending inappropriate, unfeasible, or guilt-causing urges, memories, and wishes to the unconscious, where they are out of sight, if not out of mind.

The ability to repress such thoughts is vital to the individual's ability to negotiate the pathways of life. If a child had never learned to repress the urge to kill a sibling for mother's attention, he or she would have spent years in punishment. If trauma victims could not repress the memories of the trauma, they would be caught in a loop of horrifying and painful mental activity. If mothers could not repress the pain of childbirth, the population of the world would fall to zero.

Sigmund Freud was the first to identify and define repression. Freud's conception of the mind is characterized primarily by dynamism, or the interplay of energy between the different levels of consciousness, and the interaction between the various functions of the mind. He identified the one function of the mind that brings together these various aspects as repression—the maintenance of what is and what isn't appropriately retained in the conscious mind.

According to Freud, the reason why some ideas cannot become conscious is that a certain force opposes them—otherwise they could become conscious. In psychoanalysis, the opposing force is removed and the ideas in question are made conscious. The state in which the ideas existed before being made conscious is called repression. The concept of the unconscious mind is derived from the theory of repression.

Most individuals possess a coherent organization of mental processes, which is called ego. It is to the ego that consciousness is attached; the ego controls the individual's approaches to the external world. Ego is the mental agency that supervises all its own component processes. Even though it goes to sleep at night, ego still exercises censorship on dreams. Thus, from ego proceed the repressions that seek to exclude certain ideas in the mind from consciousness and also from dreams and other activities of the mind. In classic analysis, the ideas that have been shut out stand in opposition to the ego, and the analyst is faced with the task of removing the resistances the ego displays against that which is repressed.

The timely repression of impulses and urges gives individuals the capacity to move on and meet the demands of the world. Yet repressions can become overwhelming. They can build up, causing tension, stress, and anxiety, sometimes to debilitating proportions. As the repressed ideas bob beneath the conscious surface, they sap energy because they force the individual to maintain constant lines of defense against them. Often the pressure becomes too great, and the individual finds release through some external means.

Depending on other psychological factors, a release can be benign, such as displacing the energy into physical activity, or it can be harmful. Repressed anger is generally at the root of such displacements. The individual who has repressed anger and suddenly finds release coming from uncontrollable and often unfathomable depths can react in unpredictable, sometimes unimaginable ways. We hear extreme stories of people walking into post offices or restaurants and opening fire, but lesser actions are carried out from the same depths— for example, the frustrated worker who suddenly smashes equipment on the job, the spouse who asks his or her mate for a divorce out of the blue, or the college student who suddenly drops out against expectations of academic success.

The nature of repression is that individuals are not usually aware of it. Even those who might understand and guess from unpleasurable feelings that a resistance is at work don't know what it is or how to describe it. In this opposition of the conscious and the unconscious, a standoff between the coherent ego and the repressed occurs. Sometimes the standoff can be penetrated, and sometimes other coping mechanisms and behavior modifications have to be made to ease the anguish.

Repression is evidenced in handwriting in the retracing of *m*'s, *n*'s, and *h*'s. The letters appear to be wedged together without any opening. Another indication is tight spacing of words and lines of writing.

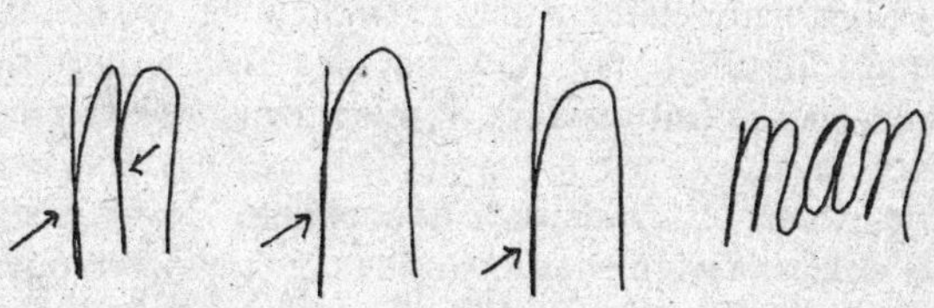

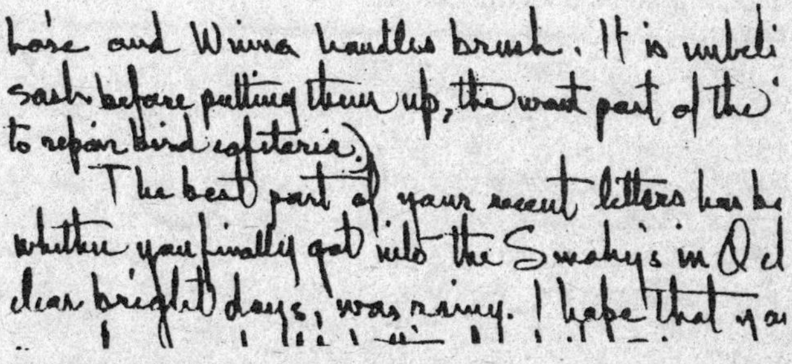

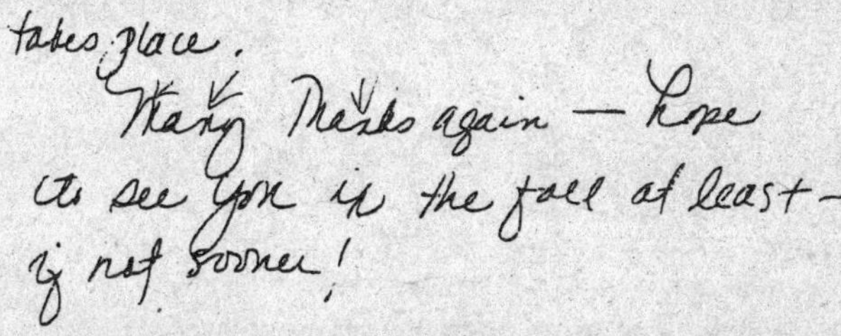

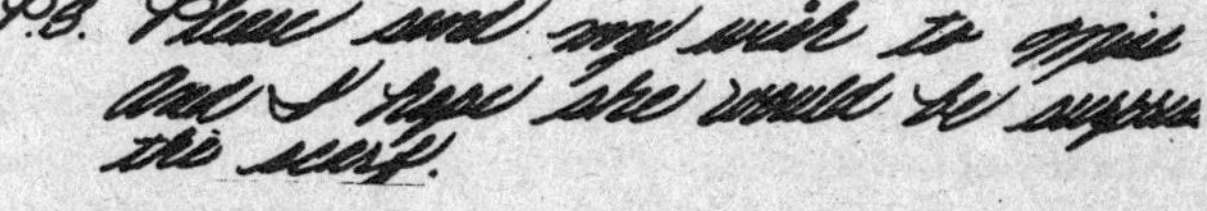

Repression is indicated by retraced *m*'s, *n*'s, and *h*'s. These samples not only have retraced *m*'s, *n*'s, and *h*'s, but also compressed letter spacing, also indicating repression.

Because repression is a profound psychological mechanism, graphotherapy does not aim to intrude itself into the delicate process. Instead, it works toward freeing self-expression, particularly to help the individual find the means to express himself or herself without fear. When this channel is freed, more positive ways of release can be explored by the individual.

The exercise takes six days to complete. On the first day, fill up at least a page with the following drawing to open up your receptivity pathways. (Doing the drawing feels freer if you use a non-smudging marker.)

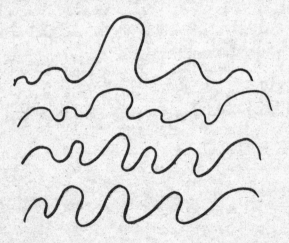

This drawing helps open receptivity pathways.

On days two and three, do a page of *m*'s, *n*'s, and *h*'s that are as open as you can make them. If you have to retrace, do the best you can to start.

m m m m

n n n n n n

h h h h h h

Be careful not to retrace *m*'s, *n*'s, and *h*'s.

On the next three days, write the following sentence:

I envision a more open and expressive manner.

Fill up a half page. Use the second half to write your thoughts on freeing yourself from repressions. Be spontaneous and, of course, careful not to retrace the upstrokes in your *m*'s, *n*'s, and *h*'s, keeping the spacing of the letters fairly wide.

Consciousness-raising groups may additionally be an ally in dealing with repression. You may also try discussing your feelings with a trusted friend, associate or family member.

Most of all, be patient. This trait can take a long time to explore and understand.

SENSITIVITY TO CRITICISM

Sensitivity to criticism is an overawareness of others' perceptions about oneself. It is fear of disapproval coupled with the need for approval. An excessive need for approval is related to low self-esteem or low self-acceptance. A person with this trait depends heavily on others for a sense of self-worth. This creates a fear of rejection that results in a heightened sensitivity to criticism (as well as difficulty saying no to the demands of others).

An excessive need for approval can also create the tendency to take responsibility for the feelings of others or to be overly sensitive to others' needs. A person with this trait often makes it his or her responsibility to keep friends and

relatives happy. Yet the irony is that the fear of negative evaluation makes these efforts fraught with anxiety.

Instead of an altruistic desire to help, stemming from the
wholeness of self, there is a fear-based drive to gain
approval, coming from a sense of lacking. People who are
sensitive to criticism may allow such fears to hinder relationships, especially where there is a tendency to take things
very personally.

In handwriting, it is shown by a wide loop in the lowercase *d* and *t* stems. The bigger the loop, the more sensitivity.

Wide loops in the *d* and *t* stems indicate sensitivity to criticism. The bottom sample belongs to Humphrey Bogart.

The exercise to help diminish sensitivity to criticism is done for five to seven consecutive days.

First, do the exercises for open-mindedness and enthusiasm. Then fill up a page with *d*'s and *t*'s that have no loops.

Next, write a page of this sentence:

Don't take matters to heart.

Keep the *d*'s and *t*'s loop-free if possible. If this is too difficult, try to keep your loops narrow.

d d d d d

t t t t t

Don't take matters to heart.

don't take matters to heart.

Write a page of *d*'s and *t*'s without loops. Then write the sentence without loops in the *d*'s and *t*'s.

Be aware of any criticisms that you mete out to others.

9
SUCCESS EXERCISES

THIS LAST GROUP OF FIVE EXERCISES IS GEARED TOWARD YOUR personal success. Each promotes strengthening a different aspect of self. Coupled with the work you've done so far, they will allow you to put yourself out in the world with confidence and the expectation that you can succeed.

GOAL SETTING

A goal is a result toward which behavior is consciously or unconsciously directed. Everyone has goals, whether they are clearly defined or not. Your objective is to be able to set meaningful goals for yourself, ones that you can attain.

Striving to meet your objectives should be as satisfying as accomplishing them. When you have goals you are able to:

- decide what is important for you to achieve in your life
- separate what is important from what is irrelevant
- motivate yourself to achieve

Goals are most effectively set by defining them positively and realistically, keeping them manageable and prioritizing them by writing them down.

Goal setting is a very powerful approach that can help you achieve strong returns in all areas of your life. At its simplest level, setting goals helps you attain what you want at the moment through short-term motivation. At a more complex level, the process gives you direction as to where you want to go in life—it provides long-term vision. It helps you focus and organize your resources. By knowing what you want to accomplish, you know where you should concentrate your energies and where you should eliminate distractions.

Effective goal setting has many benefits, including the ability to achieve more, improve performance, reduce stress and anxiety through the satisfaction of accomplishment, and, perhaps most significant, improve self-confidence. The latter is possible because the process of achieving goals and seeing their positive results gives you the self-belief you need to achieve higher and more difficult goals.

In graphology, the level of goal setting is indicated by the placement of the *t* bar on the *t* stem. The higher the *t* bar on the stem, the more challenging the goals that are set. *T* bars that are placed low on the *t* stem indicate a lack of goals. This may derive from underestimating capabilities or a lack of confidence or self-esteem.

When the bar floats over the stem, the individual has very high goals but may be a dreamer who can't make those visions come true—unless good achievement traits are found in the rest of the handwriting.

T

When the bar rests on the stem, goals are placed very high. The individual is ambitious, with the practicality to put ideals into motion.

t

Practical goals are indicated when the bar crosses the stem in the middle.

t t

Goal orientation is low when the bar crosses the stem below the middle. The lower the bar is on the stem, the lower the goal orientation.

have started to take my portfolio to agencies. It is a challenge to find the right place but it it

To Dave Gideon, with recollection of his courtesy and hospitality,
Nov 1922 Calvin Coolidge

These two samples show high goal orientation. The bottom one is from Calvin Coolidge, who wasn't seen as a dreamer but whose *t* bars show he had lofty goals.

Jane Stein was drifting through high school. She seemed to have no motivation and little interest in life. Her goals were almost nonexistent. When asked what she wanted to do when she graduated from high school, she would shrug her shoulders diffidently and respond, "I don't know." When she finally graduated, through the path of least resistance, she took a job as a sales clerk in a local discount chain store. However, what is interesting about Jane is that she's extremely bright.

Given another set of life circumstances she might have done very well in school, gone on to college, and had a satisfying career. Unfortunately, her parents were divorced; her father was mostly absent from her life, and her mother pursued her own social life when she wasn't working to provide for Jane and her two brothers. Jane's home life was not only dysfunctional, but there was no support system around her. As a result, she suffered and found little joy in life, which was reflected in her poor attitude and lack of personal objectives.

Eventually, as she began to mature and experience the world, Jane's native intelligence and strong will began to tell her that she could learn and experience more. She enrolled in a community college and took a few courses at night. She availed herself of counseling provided at the college. Her odyssey eventually brought her to one of my seminars and then to my office for private consultation. Jane came to me for six months for graphotherapy, which greatly intrigued her. She worked long and hard on her exercises, actually choosing which traits she would like to address.

Today, ten years after she graduated from high school with no prospects, Jane is motivated and feels fulfilled, working as an assistant to a psychiatrist while she is finishing her master's thesis in psychology. The proof of her successful change of attitude is here in her most recent handwriting.

High school is about to end, but I don't

Much has happened to me in the past years, and I'm at a

Jane's handwriting (top line) not only shows a lack of goal orientation, but the downward slant indicates pessimism. By contrast, her handwriting several years later (below) significantly reflects a change in attitude and goal orientation.

Begin the goal setting exercise with relaxation exercises. Proceed to the exercise for determination, which by now you have mastered. Do it again anyway to link into this exercise for goal setting. Then write a page of *t*'s with the bars placed anywhere you desire on the *t* stem but not lower than halfway down the stem. You yourself will be indicating where you want to place your goal level. You can bring your *t* bars down a bit if you feel you are flying too high, or you can edge them up if you feel that your level is too low.

If you feel that your goal level is practical, leave it alone. If your *t* bars fall below the halfway point, raise them.

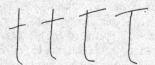

Place the *t* bar anywhere you want as long as it is above the halfway point of the *t* stem.

Now write this sentence:

Set objectives to attain.

Fill two pages. Place your *t* bars exactly where you desire them to be on the *t* stem as per the instructions above.

Enhance the graphotherapy exercise with positive reinforcement. Set small, short-term goals for yourself each day.
For example, you may make reading at least a page in a book
your objective. Make sure the goal, however small, has a positive benefit for you. Write the goal down and check it off as
completed at the end of the day. If you didn't accomplish your
goal, that's all right—just keep trying until you get results.
Then as you raise the *t* bar, set longer-range goals for yourself.

After completing each day's exercises, write how you
feel after accomplishing even the smallest goals. If there
wasn't completion, write how that felt as well. After all the
goals you set are attained, move on to the next exercise.
Watch the change in your *t* bar.

When you sign your name and date each day, be conscious of any *t*'s in your signature.

CONSISTENCY

Consistency is coherence, unity, and concurrence. The
opposite is erraticism, variability, and irregularity. Consistent behavior benefits all other positive personality traits. At
its most profound level, consistency can help you cultivate
inner peace and harmony and, in turn, a meaningful life.

Psychologically, parts of self are frequently at odds with
each other. The results are often conflict and personal strug-
gle. Cultivating consistency can help bring these two aspects
of self into alignment—into concurrence—and consequently
to inner peace and harmony where life seems more complete.
This position permits personal growth to happen on a clearer
level because you have more control over yourself through
a clearer attitude toward life. We grow through problem-
solving, and consistency allows this process to flow.

Another important benefit of consistency is the ability to
communicate coherently, itself a product of inner peace and
harmony. Consistency in the way you communicate can create an environment in which any issue can be effectively discussed because you are able to identify what you want. In
this environment, consistency can help you:

- develop better communication skills
- build trust
- improve relationships

From time to time I use graphotherapy in relationship counseling. Often one or both partners in a relationship, be it a marriage or a business partnership, can't communicate consistently. The messages being received are inharmonious and mixed. When partners in a relationship learn not to send mixed messages, when the communication becomes consistent, there is usually a great leap forward to resolving problems. Consistency helps put you on the same page as those you are dealing with.

In handwriting, consistency is called an evaluated trait, meaning that it's determined by a set of variables. These include the slant of the writing, the spacing between lines, letters and words, the height and width of strokes, and the rhythm of writing. It can also be seen in the spatial use of the writing field and in the evenness of the base line on which the writing rests.

I have also noticed a dramatic change in my personal relationships. I have become more open, and I have developed effective communication skills.

No man has earned the right to intellectual ambition until he has learned to lay his course by a star he has never seen ——

These two samples show consistency; both look "even" and balanced.

To cultivate consistency, practice these form drawings. (These drawings are also excellent for developing determination and follow-through.)

These forms help you develop consistency as well as determination and follow-through. Ideally, the "single" set of forms should be drawn in the morning, and the mirror-image forms should be executed in the evening.

Do this exercise as often as you like, whenever you feel the need to develop this trait. It is helpful to do the exercise in conjunction with the exercise for confusion. Together they encourage clarity and harmony in thinking. This exercise is also excellent for helping to develop goals and is especially effective with the exercise for determination.

SELF-CONFIDENCE

Self-confidence can't be discussed without relating it to self-esteem, the way you value yourself. Individuals with self-esteem usually seek the challenge and stimulation of what they perceive as worthwhile or demanding goals.

Being self-confident means you are sure of yourself to the extent that you are able to establish goals that are achievable. Because they have conviction in themselves, individuals with self-confidence expect to attain those goals. In turn, reaching the goals nurtures healthy self-esteem.

By contrast, low self-esteem seeks the safety of the familiar and undemanding, which in turn further weakens self-esteem and self-confidence. Both paths are self-reinforcing and self-perpetuating.

Self-confidence helps individuals to achieve and to cope better with adversity when it befalls them. The higher the self-confidence, the more ambitious a person is in experiencing life—emotionally, intellectually, creatively, and spiritually. Self-confidence permits more open, honest, and appropriate communications—there is no muddiness or evasiveness because there is no uncertainty about the individual's own thoughts and feelings, or fear of the listener's response.

Self-confidence also inclines a person to positive relationships in which respect, benevolence, good will, and fairness prevail. Self-confident individuals don't tend to perceive others as a threat, so self-respect becomes the foundation of respect for others. Thus, people with good self-confidence don't interpret relationships in adversarial terms, nor do they approach them with expectations of rejection, humiliation, or betrayal.

A well-developed sense of self-confidence equates to kindness, generosity, social cooperation, and personal happiness. Self-confidence ultimately is self-knowledge of your own personal power.

In your handwriting, self-confidence is related to your aspirations, which are shown in the height you place your *t* bars on the *t* stem and also in the way you write them—large versus small. The size of your capital *I* is also a strong indication of your self-confidence.

T t I l

I have to go to Paris

I am not too concerned about

Self-confidence is shown in the placement of the *t* bar
on the stem and in the height of your capital letters relative to the size of the lowercase letters.

Joan Jameson was the editor of her high school newspaper. She loved to write and so planned a career in journalism. But as her college years progressed, she began to feel
increasing anxiety about her career choice. Yet she knew she
really didn't want to do anything else, either. Joan's handwriting was full of creative talent and writing ability, along
with the analytical ability a journalist needs to probe a story.
What was missing, however, was self-confidence, which in
journalism can be a major stumbling block. It became apparent that Joan dreaded interviewing strangers and couldn't
manage the assertiveness necessary to ask hard questions
and pursue a story. She feared rebuff and the prospect of
making a fool of herself with unprofessional questions.
Working on Joan's self-confidence helped her overcome
these fears, graduate with honors, and secure a job on a
major newspaper as a beat reporter.

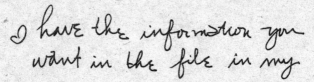

Joan's handwriting shows a lack of self-confidence, although many other traits, such as literary ability and creativity, are present.

The exercise for building self-confidence takes ten days to complete. Start the exercise by doing the enthusiasm and open-mindedness exercises. Then, for three days, write a half page of *t*'s on lined paper. Cross the stem in the middle, which indicates practical goals.

Fill the rest of the page with this sentence, watching your *t*'s and placing the bars in the middle of the stem:

I understand what I want to attain.

On the fourth day, continue as before but switch to unlined paper and this sentence:

I set these objectives with intent.

Do this phase of the exercise for another three days.

t t t t t t t t t t t

I set these objectives with intent.

I set these objectives with intent.

All of the *t*'s should have strong *t* bars placed aross the middle of the *t* stem.

Then, for the next two days, on unlined paper, write a half page of *t*'s with the bar crossed high.

Write a sentence of your choosing on the other half of the paper. Express your feelings about your change of goals and what that will mean to you.

T T T T t
T T t t t

Write a sentence that you choose.

Write these *t*'s with the bar placed high on the stem.

On the final day, write and print larger capital *I*'s than you usually make; the *I* should be at least twice the size of your lowercase letters. Gradually bring the *I*'s down in size but still keep them large.

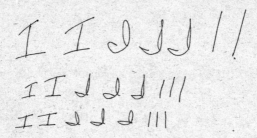

Large *I*'s help you focus on the self-confident you.

On all ten days, after the specified exercise, fill a sheet of unlined paper with this drawing. Each triangle represents a higher level of self-confidence. Start the triangles very large and, after four days, vary the sizes.

The triangles represent levels of self-confidence.

INTEGRITY

Integrity is the integration of ideals, convictions, standards, beliefs, and behavior. It can be defined from several points of view. On a moralistic level, it is righteousness, virtue, and goodness. From a law and order perspective, it is honesty. From a broader, societal point of view, it is soundness, principle, and honor. In all cases, the standards for integrity are defined by a culture's mores and value structure. When behavior is consistent with society's values—when ideals and practice match—a person is said to have integrity.

As a person matures, he or she absorbs and develops standards promulgated by society, parents, and other authority or support structures. In the process, a self-concept of personal integrity develops, which can have profound effects on behavior. Barring sociopathic tendencies, those who behave in ways that conflict with their own assessment of what is appropriate lose face in their own eyes. Eventually, they may trust themselves less or cease to trust themselves at all. The conflict may be subconscious or exist on some level of consciousness. In any case, self-esteem is wounded. Lapses of integrity are detrimental to self-esteem because they are betrayals of personal convictions.

Hypocrisy is a typical lapse of integrity. The individual who says one thing and does the other is not only acting against his or her own better judgment, but by its nature, is self-invalidating. The hypocrite has no credibility. Lapses of integrity are undermining and debasing to one's sense of self. They can manifest in many ways, including feelings of guilt and shame, anxiety, depression, and insomnia. Character development is an important cornerstone of a healthy society. We need principles to guide our lives, for integrity is one of the guardians of mental health.

The indications of a low integrity level in handwriting are shown by stroke formations called double loops. A loop on the left side of an *o* or *a* represents self-deceit. On the right side it represents secrecy. When both loops are present (double loops), the individual is engaging in some level of deception, from simply seeing the world as conforming to his or her own specification, to out-and-out duplicity.

Other traits in the handwriting, such as withdrawal, defiance, and shallowness, help define a person's lack of integrity.

peace on earth

green is my favorite color

I have reached the

Double loops are indicative of poor integrity. These samples indicate lapses in integrity, with the two samples on the bottom being more serious than the others.

Lapses of integrity are not always obvious but have their effect. Sam Johnson is an insurance salesman who lives on commissions. He has a terrific aptitude for selling and has been very successful in his career. Sam's trouble started when his company began an incentive program, which included cruises, holidays, and other rewards for high-dollar-volume sales. Sam found himself using his skills to sell clients insurance they didn't really need. Sam began to suffer from insomnia and a general health breakdown. Suddenly he felt tired all the time and got more colds than he'd ever had before.

Sam said to me, "I've got a great life—wonderful kids, a

devoted wife, and every material comfort I want. I don't know what's the matter with me." Yet Sam *did* know what was bothering him. Deep down he knew he was violating his own principles. Eventually, Sam admitted how duplicitous he had become. He asked me how I saw deceit in handwriting. I showed Sam the double loops, but later, when he tried to eliminate them from his writing, he found the task impossible. Through handwriting *and* counseling, I was able to help Sam restore his integrity.

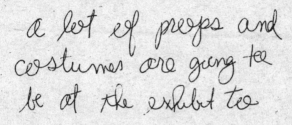

Sam's writing shows telltale double loops.

You can help keep your integrity sound by first doing the exercises for self-reliance, and then for concentration, which will help you build discipline and self-control. Next, for four consecutive days, start with a set of relaxation exercises and then fill a page of lined paper with *o*'s that are clear and round and have no loops in them. Switch to unlined paper on days five through eight.

This exercise is not an easy one to do and may take longer than most, so if you feel you would like to repeat it, do so until you are satisfied with the results.

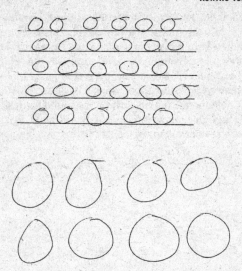

Keep o's clear and full to promote integrity.

SELF-RELIANCE

Self-reliance is a basic trust in oneself. It can't exist without some level of self-esteem and, most important, self-acceptance. At the deepest level, self-reliance is commitment to the value of one's own person, the primary act of self-value that serves as the basis for self-trust.

Self-reliance is the willingness to rely on oneself without denial or evasion. Self-reliance is also the refusal to regard any part of self, no matter what it is—thoughts, actions, dreams, beliefs—as alien, as "not me." Therefore, it is the willingness to experience and take ownership of the self.

Self-reliance is to be in partnership with self, rather than in an adversarial relationship, and to be able to accept all thoughts, emotions, or behaviors as expressions of self, even if those expressions are ones that you don't like or admire. Thus, when confronted with mistakes or poor choices, in accepting them as our own you are able to learn from them and do better in the future. Self-reliance permits a willingness to confront rather than run away from and evade the challenges of life and to strive for command. The self-reliant individual seeks to be independent and to make up his or her own mind after listening to others.

Self-esteem is a component of self-reliance. It is having self-respect and a sound self-image of yourself. It means you have a well-developed sense of worth, which permits you to relate to your environment with purposefulness. It is also knowing you deserve happiness. Individuals with good self-esteem have a realistic confidence in themselves. They feel secure within themselves and tend to view the world as open to them.

Self-esteem energizes and motivates. How people experience themselves influences every moment of their existence. This self-evaluation is the basic context in which people act and react, choose values, set goals, and generally navigate through life. Responses to events are shaped in great part by who and what people think they are and how worthy they perceive themselves to be.

Of all the judgments made in life, none is more important than the judgment passed on the self.

Self-esteem is a basic human need that is indispensable to healthy development; it also has importance for survival. Positive self-esteem provides the capacity for strength and regeneration. When self-esteem is low, resilience in the face of life is diminished. Such individuals may crumble where others overcome. They may also be more likely to live their lives to avoid pain rather than to experience joy. This is not to say that everyone with low self-esteem fails. Individuals may still have the talent and drive to achieve a great deal in spite of a poor self-concept. For example, productive workaholics may be driven to achieve to prove their worth. For the most part, though, individuals with low self-esteem tend to be less effective and less creative than they potentially could be and less likely to find satisfaction in their achievements. Nothing they do ever seems to be enough.

Research shows that one of the best ways to have good self-esteem is to have parents with healthy self-esteem. Children who have the best chance of developing healthy self-esteem have parents who:

- raise them with love and respect
- convey to them that they are wanted and accepted
- set reasonable limits and establish reasonable rules
- have appropriate expectations of them
- are consistent, not contradictory
- do not ridicule or humiliate
- don't try to control them

However, the result of positive parenting is not inevitable. Research also shows that children raised by these standards may still become insecure, self-doubting adults. Conversely, many people emerge from alarming backgrounds, and go on to have a powerful sense of their own value and dignity. To this extent, little is known about the genetic or biological factors that influence self-esteem.

Self-esteem and self-image are represented in the personal pronoun *I*. People with a sound self-image and good self-esteem write their *I*'s about two and a half times the height of the small letters.

I feel great Today

This sample shows good self-esteem in the height of the capital *I* in relation to lowercase letters.

Self-reliance is shown in handwriting primarily by underlined signatures:

(Top to bottom) Founding Fathers John Hancock and Benjamin Franklin, and actress and writer Cornelia Otis Skinner, all show excellent self-reliance. In the case of Franklin and Hancock, this quality helped immeasurably in the founding of the United States of America.

Nancy Osborne's problems had been severe since adolescence. She had tried many forms of therapy, traditional and nontraditional, without result. For a time she'd even been a member of a so-called cult, in the hopes that an intense religious affiliation would help her. In her younger years she'd also tried drugs. At forty-three, Nancy arrived at my office not convinced that I could help her but desperate to try in any case. Nancy's handwriting contained a lot of repression as well as low self-esteem and anger. As it turned out, Nancy was the product of emotionally abusive parents. Without a background of love, respect, and nurturing, she lacked any belief in herself. She considered herself a loser who wouldn't amount to much, which is what her parents constantly told her. How could she believe it wasn't so?

The graphotherapy program tailored for Nancy's needs began to open her eyes. I helped Nancy strengthen her strong traits first, so that she could cope with the tougher work ahead. As I do with many clients, such as Celia Joff, our sessions were taped, and on that tape I included instructions for her—exercises to do in between our meetings. I included exercises such as determination, optimism, open-mindedness, and concentration.

Nancy and I have been working together for two years. Her deep problems have been considerably alleviated. There is more to do, but at least now Nancy no longer believes she was destined to fail. Nancy has improved her life dramatically and knows she has the means now to keep on improving it.

I make a pumpkin pie with

Nancy's writing reflects poor self-image.

Rick Hewlett was sent to me by his parents, who were extremely concerned about their son's future. Rick was a business major who had just entered his senior year in college. Not too far down the road would be final exams, job interviews, and preparation for the world outside of academia. Apparently Rick wasn't looking forward to any of this, for when I saw him he was a bundle of nerves. It was obvious that he was under a great deal of stress, so we worked on relaxation exercises. Next, we dealt with the underlying reason for his problem, which was a lack of self-reliance. Rick was sure he'd fail once he got into the world and had to stand out there alone. He didn't trust himself to make the right decisions and feared the consequences of perceived wrong action. After three months of intensive graphotherapy, Rick not only was able to calm down but also made significant strides in believing in himself. Rick is still working on self-reliance, but his problem is no longer debilitating, and now he has the proper tools to work with.

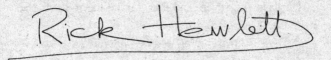

Rick's self-image was strengthened by having him under-line his signature.

Here is the exercise for self-reliance and self-esteem. It takes eight days to complete.

On day one, write a half page of your signature, sloping up. Then fill the rest of the page with your signature, sloping up and underlined once.

On days two and three, write a full page of your signature, sloping up, and underscore each twice. Press down harder than usual when you draw the lines.

On days four and five, write the signature connecting the underscores to the end of the last letter in your name. The underscore should first veer to the left and then return to the right.

your signature

your signature

your signature

As you execute the various underscores, make sure to keep the lines sloping upward.

On days six, seven, and eight, write the following sentence:

I trust myself and accept myself.

Sign your name and underline it after each statement.

You may also want to do the following in conjunction with the instructions above. Every day, fill half a page of unlined paper with *I*'s that stand tall and vertical and are simply straight lines. If you naturally slant to the right, have the *I*'s slant as well.

Next, fill up the rest of the page with cursive or Roman *I*'s, starting out very large and diminishing in size to your usual writing style.

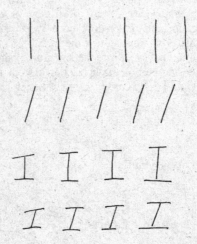

Practice writing *I*'s this way to boost self-image.

In your notebook, record your feelings as you worked the exercise, particularly noting how you felt about the underscoring. Was this part of the process comfortable?

When you feel that you have satisfactorily completed this exercise, try to include underscoring daily, such as your signature or words you feel moved to emphasize as you write.

10
FIND YOUR COMFORT ZONE AND
STAY OFF THE THERAPIST'S COUCH

EVERY ONE OF US LIVES IN SOME DEFINED AREA THAT CAN BE termed as a personal comfort zone—the area in which life is unstressed. Outside this boundary lie the challenges and obstacles as well as the potentials and possibilities of life. But it is an illusion that the boundary keeps these outer influences separate from us. The trick is not to use the comfort zone to hide in but instead to regard it as a home base from which to navigate the pathways of life.

The idea of a comfort zone originated in the heating and air conditioning trade. It's ideally 72° Fahrenheit, where neither heat nor air conditioning is necessary to be comfortable. A little warmer and you're likely to turn on the air conditioning, and a little colder and you'll put on the heat. The human mind works much the same way. Each of us has internal comfort settings by which we tend to operate and regulate our behavior.

The comfort zone is often why good intentions are never realized and resolutions fall by the wayside. The comfort zone is why change can be so difficult. To adjust your comfort zone, you need only change the settings of your mind. If, for example, you change your idea of how you should live, you will soon change how you do live.

The process of change is uncomfortable. Discomfort is not a symptom that something is wrong; it's a symptom that something is right. Your discomfort is telling you that change is necessary. Learn to expect the discomfort of change and embrace it as proof that you have the capacity to grow. Cultivate change; accept discomfort; insist on growth. When you do, your comfort zone will expand to fill up your world.

We've come a long way together from the time you read the first words of *Rewrite Your Life*. Now it's time for you to take the whole body of knowledge I've given you, and measure your progress in the real world. You are a stronger and more confident person than when you began this book. Your mission is to continue to test yourself as you navigate the course of life. Are you better able to handle situations now than you were before? Do you feel more comfortable doing so? If you can answer yes to these questions, you have already begun to find your true comfort zone.

Your true comfort zone is the place you create that permits you to function harmoniously and successfully. It is the platform from which you can continue to improve and grow and find the best in yourself. With the knowledge you now possess, you can continue to strive to reach new goals and new potentials and widen your circle of comfort.

Life should be a continuous improvement process, and this means that graphotherapy doesn't stop at the last page of this book. Graphotherapy is an ongoing process you can keep learning from. The work begun here is just a start. Keep it going and make graphotherapy part of your lifestyle, because using it can enhance every part of your life. This I know from experience, and I hope you know it by now too. You can find your true path and stay on it with graphotherapy.

Successful graphotherapy should always end in fulfillment for both therapist and client, a fact that I find most gratifying. I'm never so happy as when I see someone I've been able to help move forward into the world equipped with a new set of skills and the confidence and self-aware-ness to make a difference in life.

This is what I hope you come away with as you complete this book. I want you to apply the knowledge you've gained through our relationship to make your life more fulfilling than it has ever been before. You now have all the tools you need to enjoy an improved quality of life. The resource of graphotherapy can help you over any rough spots you encounter in the future, will lead you to success, and is your constant ally in finding the best in yourself.

Appendix 1
Frequently Asked Questions

People often ask me questions about graphology and graphotherapy. Here are some that are most frequently asked.

How do I know that graphology is valid?

Most people aren't aware that handwriting is "brainwriting", and some find it difficult to believe, therefore, that handwriting has any credibility as a psychological, personality assessment, or therapeutic tool. Over the years, much research has been conducted to prove the validity of graphology, both to enhance the status of graphology as a profession, and to better understand the exact scientific principles of it, especially in establishing objective benchmarks for consistency and reliability.

The elements of handwriting—the strokes, the form, the slant, and the size—are all measurable, and provide the platform for validation. Serious validation studies have been ongoing since the late nineteenth century. The results have continually provided more and more insight into graphology (and graphotherapy) as findings have been built upon findings, as breakthroughs in the understanding of the human brain and physiology have occurred, and as technology has advanced.

Some early studies simply sought to establish guidelines through finding consistencies empirically, that is, by analyzing and comparing literally hundreds and hundreds of hand-writing samples. Later studies have used methodologies which include determining scales based on measurable elements, such as the rhythm exhibited in muscular movements, and analyzing the information to produce statistical evidence.

More contemporary studies use computers and advance statistical modeling to measure and set benchmarks for consistency, and to further compare the results against already established and traditional approaches to graphology and graphotherapy.

Is graphology an art or a science?

It is both and can be likened to the art-science of psychology. Graphology itself is a science, because the body of knowledge permits future deduction and consistent evaluation. It is also an art because it requires the graphologist to make certain judgments in assessing a handwriting sample.

What is the difference between graphology and graphotherapy?

A professional graphologist is trained in the interpretation of handwriting patterns and their relationship to the personality. Graphologists work mainly by drawing up a profile of personality traits based on a thorough study of a handwriting sample.

A graphotherapist is trained in graphology and has additional training in psychology. A graphotherapist guides a client in altering handwriting patterns as a means of removing negative thought habits and replacing them with positive, self-supportive ones.

Is there such a thing as bad handwriting?

There is no "good" or "bad" handwriting. These are perceptions or value judgments with no foundation in the science of graphology or graphotherapy. There is only who you are and what you do.

What if I don't really believe graphotherapy will make a difference?

Although you do yourself a disservice by being negative, this belief has nothing to do with altering thought patterns through changing handwriting. Our thought habits are reflected in the neurological patterns in the brain. By altering the way we write, we alter the way we think, and the neurological pathways shift accordingly.

What's wrong with the way I learned to write?

In the United States, most children are taught handwriting methods that were developed more than one hundred years ago. These systems (Palmer and Zaner–Bloser) are not only out of sync with modern times but actually contain negative traits, such as jealousy loops. Everyone should not have to learn to write in one style.

What if I like my handwriting and don't want to change it?

That's fine. If there are traits in your handwriting that you feel warrant change, doing the exercises will not force change that you don't want. As you change of your own will, your handwriting automatically follows suit to reflect this.

Does being left-handed or right-handed matter?

Since handwriting is brainwriting, there is no effect on the interpretation, regardless of whether the writer is left-handed or right-handed—or even if the writing is done by a disabled person by foot or mouth. It's the brain that wills the handwriting to look a certain way.

Can I fake my writing and fool the graphologist?

You can't unless you are a very good forger, but even forgers get tired. Someone who tries to forge a style of handwriting has to fight against his or her own stamina. With tiredness or tenseness comes the revelation of the true self.

Appendix 2
The History of Graphotherapy

Nearly four hundred years ago, in a university in Bologna, Italy, a man named Camillo Baldi worked to understand ancient manuscripts buried away in the old library of the university. Baldi, a doctor of medicine and philosophy at the university, through his interest, his research, his persistence, and above all, his love of a good mystery, became the first person on record to "rediscover" and undertake the study of graphology in the modern era. Like so many before him, and many yet to come, Baldi was interested in the relationship between handwriting and the writer, but in the early seventeenth century, when Baldi lived, graphology was nearly dead. What the doctor did was give new life to a science that had gone underground and been well hidden in the Dark Ages.

Camillo Baldi laid open this concealed subject and initiated ongoing research into it. This act was extremely important, for his work added to the scientific body of knowledge of his time, became part of the great thinking of the Enlightenment, and spawned serious examination of the science of handwriting analysis.

The earliest known records of handwriting analysis are found in the commentaries of the Romans, notably in the chronicles of the historian Suetonius, who wrote that Caesar Augustus did not separate his words (in writing) or carry excess letters over to the next line of script. In ancient Greece, Aristotle commented on the benefits of handwriting analysis, noting that just as no two individuals have the same speech pattern, they don't have the same style of handwriting. And in China, about one thousand years ago, some rudiments of handwriting analysis were known. The eleventh century philosopher and painter Kuo Jo Hsu maintained that handwriting could unfailingly show if a person was vulgar or of noble thought and mind.

As Christianity began to envelop the Western world, the church became the seat of knowledge in the West. Consequently, the scholarship and study of handwriting and writing analysis became the domain of the priesthood. Eventually, graphology, along with other valuable knowledge, was disenfranchised in the Dark Ages, surviving only because certain monks wanted to protect the knowledge and keep it for themselves. Yet, as difficult as the monks made it, graphology was still being practiced in 1622, the period of discovery that foreshadowed the Enlightenment, when Baldi brought the hidden knowledge to light once again.

Despite Baldi's research into handwriting analysis, and despite the publication of a book on his studies, investigation into the field, although revitalized, sputtered along in fits and starts until the nineteenth century. It was at this time, in France, that graphology began to be studied with consistency and with continued scientific attention. The momentum, once begun, gathered.

From France, interest spread to Germany, Hungary, and Switzerland, in particular. In the early nineteenth century the Bishop of Amiens, the Archbishop of Cambrai, and the abbe Louis Flandrin held regular discussions on the subject of handwriting analysis. It was, in fact, either the abbe Flandrin or his pupil, the abbe Jean-Hypolite Michon, who coined the word *graphology*. It is the abbe Michon, and his own pupil, Jules Crépieux-Jamin, who are credited with the first meaningful systemization of handwriting analysis. Together, they matched isolated symbols to character traits. Michon alone collected thousands of handwriting samples over a forty-year period and eventually founded the Society of Graphology in Paris in 1871.

Later, the French psychologist Alfred Binet, who developed IQ tests, also conducted graphological experiments and was convinced that handwriting analysis had potential as a technique for personality testing.

In 1904 in Germany, Ludwig Klages, a philosopher, put forth the theory that handwriting is an expressive movement, similar to gait, facial movement, and gesturing, which he said are all elements of the quality of rhythm. Klages believed that personality could be examined by evaluating the degrees of rhythm present in a person.

In the United States, psychologist June Downey worked with Klage's theory, and in Switzerland, graphologist Max Pulver extended the theory of rhythm to include the concept of depth. Pulver also studied the decorative flourishes in handwriting and tried to interpret them as symbols in relation to psychoanalytic theory.

During this period, graphology remained largely a European activity. American psychologists, repelled by the extravagant claims made by irresponsible graphologists, either ignored or disparaged handwriting analysis. By 1940 the migration to the United States of European graphologists trained in psychology resulted in a closer alliance between psychologists and graphologists for research purposes. The clinical applications of graphology were also expanded. Similar developments occurred in Great Britain.

Because of these important studies, and many others conducted during the nineteenth century, graphology became an accepted science in Europe, where, for instance, it is often a required course for education and psychology majors. Graphology is also much used in hiring in Europe, particularly France, where it is virtually impossible to get a job without having a graphological assessment done.

In the early part of this century, as a body of graphological knowledge began to be formed and scientifically proved, researchers realized that the brain–hand connection is actually a two-way street. If information can travel from the brain to the hand, then why should it not be possible for information to flow from the hand to the brain? It was thus that graphotherapy was born and research began on the "change your handwriting, change your life" theory.

Graphotherapy was first demonstrated in 1908 at the Paris Academy of Medicine. However, it wasn't until the late 1920s that the term *graphotherapy* came into use, again at the Paris Academy. Here, Dr. Edgar Berillon, a psychologist and specialist in mental disorders, had formulated a treatment based on the conduit established between the brain and hand via the cortex of the brain. Dr. Berillon maintained that imprinting qualities between graphological gestures and the brain were reversible. His treatment, which he termed *psychotherapie graphique*, combined both mental and physical processes. Berillon's treatment was clinically tested at the Sorbonne between 1929 and 1931 by Dr. Pierre Janet and Professor Charles Henry.

Another of the earliest proponents of graphotherapy was Paul de Sainte Colombe, founder of the Graphotherapeutics Foundation bearing his name. Sainte Colombe held degrees from the University of Paris and had been a participant in the seminal research conducted on graphotherapy. In 1966 he wrote *GraphoTherapeutics: Pen and Pencil Therapy*, which is still a classic in the field.

These are only a few of the most important early graphotherapy pioneers, but by no means the only explorers on the path. They are of a body of investigators who observed people and their handwriting, saw what was unique, and took the facts and extrapolated them into theories. Their work has been taken up and continued by others to this day.

Appendix 3
Further Reading

Baruch, Nero, ed. *Scientific Aspects of Graphology*. Thomas, 1986.

Beyerstein, Dale and Barry. *The Write Stuff*. Prometheus Books, 1992.

The Concise Graphology Notebook. W. Foulsham, 1988.

Driver, Russell, and Cathy Bryant, eds. *British Institute of Graphologists: 10th Anniversary Symposium at Kings College*. Hampton Hill, 1993.

Greene, James, and David Lewis. *The Hidden Language of Your Handwriting*. Pan Books, 1996.

Hargreaves, Gloria. *Dictionary of Doodles*. W. Foulsham, 1988.

Hartford, Huntington. *You Are What You Write*. Macmillan, 1973.

Hoosain, Rumjahn, Henry Kao, and Gerard Van Galen, eds. *Graphonomics: Contemporary Research on Handwriting*. Elsevier Science Publishing, 1986.

Jansen, Abraham. *Validation of Graphological Judgments*. Mouton, 1973.

Kurtz, Sheila. *Handwriting Analysis for Lovers and Other Significant People*. Dell, 1996.

Kurtz, Sheila, with Marilyn Lester. *Graphotypes: A New Slant on Handwriting Analysis*. Crown, 1984.

Miller, James. *Bibliography of Handwriting Analysis*. Whitson Publishing, 1982.

Nezos, Renna. *Advanced Graphology*. Scriptor Books, 1993.

Olyanova, Nadya. *The Psychology of Handwriting*. Sterling Publishing, 1961.

Rexford, John. *What Handwriting Indicates: An Analytical Graphology*. Putnam, 1904.

Roman, Clara. *Encyclopedia of the Written Word*. Ingar Publishing, 1968.

Sara, Dorothy. *Personality and Penmanship: A Guide to Handwriting Analysis*. HC Publishers, 1969.

Saudek, Robert. *Experiments With Handwriting*. Books for Professionals, 1978.

Schweighofer, Fritz. *Graphology and Psychoanalysis: The Handwriting of Sigmund Freud and His Circle*. Springer-Verlag, 1979.

Singer, Eric. *Personality in Handwriting*. 2d ed. Gerard Duckworth, 1974.

Thumm, Magdalene. *Psychology and Pathology of Handwriting*. Fowler and Wells, 1905.

FOR MORE INFORMATION

Congratulations! You've completed the exercises and have made great strides toward turning your life around. In other words, you have been your own therapist. What's more, you have this resource of graphotherapy as a tool that will stand you in good stead over a lifetime. I encourage you to continue graphotherapy in the years to come.

If you'd like more information on graphology, graphotherapy, or the development of low-cost computer-based handwriting analysis programs for personal development, you can contact me at:

The Graphology Consulting Group
80 Fifth Avenue
Suite 701
New York, NY 10011
212/807-9797

Index

Page numbers of illustrations appear in italics.